Level B

Writing Workshop

Senior Series Consultant
Beverly Ann Chin
Professor of English
University of Montana
Missoula, MT

Series Consultant
Frederick J. Panzer, Sr.
English Dept. Chair, Emeritus
Christopher Columbus High School
Miami, FL

Series Editor
Phyllis Goldenberg

 **Sadlier**

Acknowledgments

Every good faith effort has been made to locate the owners of copyrighted material to arrange permission to reprint selections. Thanks to the following for permission to reprint copyrighted material.

p. 93 "Without Warning, Molasses in January Surged Over Boston," by Edwards Park, originally appeared in *Smithsonian* 14 number 8 (November 1983), pages 213–230.

Credits

Cover Art and Design

William H. Sadlier, Inc. and Studio Montage

Interior Photos

iStockphoto.com/Ralf Broskvar: 50; DenGuy: 93; Dave Hughes: 34; Chris Schmidt: 5; Vasiliki Varvaki: 80; Jupiter Images/Photos.com: 39. Under license from Shutterstock.com/Arieliona: 86; Artpose Adam Borkowski: 78; Andi Berger: 26; BestPhotoStudio: 81; Engin Hakki Bilgin: 55; Black Russian Studio: 13; Heather A. Craig: 67; djgis: 74; FloridaStock: 105; Ronnie Howard: 23; iofoto: 7, 42, 72; Eric Isselée: 52; Jut: 18; Jason Kasumovic: 36; Robyn Mackenzie: 31; Byron W. Moore: 20; Shawn Pecor: 28; Thomas M. Perkins: 83; Larry St. Pierre: 62; serrnovik: 107; Elisei Shafer: 30; Christophe Testi: 45; Thomas Trojanowski: 15, 35; Jaren Jai Wicklund: 37.

Dear Student,

Whether you are writing an essay for school or writing an e-mail to a friend, you can only get your message across if you write clearly and correctly. *Writing Workshop* can help you improve your writing skills in an interesting and easy-to-understand way.

Writing Workshop begins by introducing you to the basics. First, you'll learn how to write **clear and effective sentences.** After you master the structure of sentences, you'll move on to writing **paragraphs.** Finally, you'll learn how to produce many different **types of writing** that you'll need to use in school, on tests, and in life. In addition, you will learn how to write for **different purposes,** such as to explain, persuade, describe, entertain, and convey an experience. This way, you will be prepared for any writing assignment that comes your way.

Don't worry. *Writing Workshop* will guide you along the way, offering **tips and clear instructions** that tell you exactly what to do and how to do it. For example, grammar tips remind you about important grammar rules and provide easy-to-understand explanations. **Tech Tips** guide you for writing on computers. Also, the writing workshop chapters end with a complete **Writing Model** that shows you exactly what a strong essay looks like.

Throughout the book, you'll have plenty of opportunities **to practice** each new skill you learn. As this program will show you, writing doesn't have to be done alone. Many activities will ask you to work with a **partner or in a small group.** As you develop your skills, **writing prompt** activities allow you to show off your writing and put to use the techniques you have learned.

Writing Workshop will give you a strong set of writing skills that you can use in school and throughout your life. With *Writing Workshop*, you'll become a better and more confident writer.

Good Luck!
The Authors

CONTENTS

CONTENTS *continued*

THE WRITING PROCESS

PREWRITING

Finding an Idea

- Freewrite or brainstorm ideas for a topic.
- Choose and narrow a topic.
- Gather details in a list or a graphic organizer.

Making a Plan

- Define your purpose.
- Know your audience.
- Put your details in order.

DRAFTING

- Concentrate on getting your ideas down—*not* on fixing errors!
- Keep your reader in mind as you write.
- Write a complete beginning, middle, and end.

REVISING

- Review your draft, looking for ways to improve it.
- As you review your draft, focus on five of the six traits of good writing (ideas and content, organization, sentence fluency, word choice, and voice).
- Ask a peer reviewer to give feedback on your draft.

EDITING AND PROOFREADING

- Look for mistakes in the sixth trait of good writing, conventions (grammar, usage, mechanics, and spelling).
- Proofread your draft one last time.

PUBLISHING AND PRESENTING

- Write a final version of your paper.
- Share your writing with your audience.

Writers at Work

Writing will help you achieve your goals in school, work, and life. Skilled writers get better grades, express their thoughts more clearly, and persuade others to agree with them.

When you write for an audience, use the five stages of the writing process: prewriting, drafting, revising, editing and proofreading, and publishing and presenting.

LESSON ① Prewriting

> ★ **When you prewrite, you consider your task, purpose, and audience. Then you choose your topic and gather details.**

Tip

At any stage of the writing process, you can go back to an earlier step to improve your writing.

Questions to Ask While Prewriting

✔ **Task:** What am I creating—a paragraph, an essay, a report, an e-mail, a story, a poem, or something else?

✔ **Purpose:** Do I want to explain something to someone, persuade someone to take action, describe a process, entertain someone by being humorous or scary, or convey or communicate an experience?

✔ **Audience:** Who will read my writing? What does my audience already know about my topic?

The next step is **choosing a topic.** Writing is easier and more fun if you choose a topic that truly interests you.

Ways to Choose Your Topic

- **Freewriting:** Spend three to five minutes writing down anything that comes into your mind. Don't worry about grammar or spelling.

- **Clustering and Listing:** Record your thoughts in a graphic organizer (such as a cluster diagram) or in a list.

- **Brainstorming:** Work with others to ask questions about a topic.

Freewriting Model

Need to think of a topic for an essay on American history—want to write about something or someone unusual, unknown. I wonder what life would have been like if I lived in a different time, but when? Colonial period? I saw tools and clothes from back then at the museum. I wonder what it was like to be my age in colonial times. What would I have worn? What was school like? What did kids do for fun?

Cluster Diagram

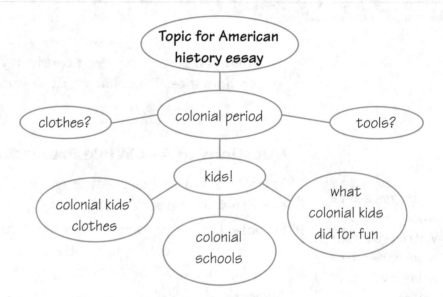

During the prewriting stage, **narrow** your topic to make it more specific and manageable. In the model above, notice how the writer starts with a broad topic and continues to increasingly narrow topics.

Topic Checklist

✔ Can I clearly sum up my topic in one sentence? (Here is an example: "My topic is games and hobbies of colonial children.")

✔ Is the topic appropriate for the length of writing that I am doing?

✔ Am I truly interested in this topic? If not, I should go back to the beginning of the prewriting stage and choose a different one.

Once you narrow your topic, you can **gather details.**

Ways to Gather Details

- Think about what you already know about your topic and what you want to find out.

- Use the clustering method to organize your information.

- Find more information by checking an encyclopedia, accessing the Internet, or talking with an expert.

Activity A **Use a separate sheet of paper to complete each item. Do the first two items individually, and get together with a small group of classmates to complete the third item. Remember to narrow your topic as you prewrite.**

1. Situation: Your science teacher wants you and three classmates to make a brochure that persuades people to recycle. Type of Prewriting: Brainstorming

2. Situation: Your teacher wants you to write an essay that describes your favorite meal. Type of Prewriting: Freewriting

3. Situation: Your social studies teacher wants you to write a report on a person in American history. Type of Prewriting: Cluster diagram

Activity B **On a separate sheet of paper, create a list or a cluster diagram for one of the broad topics below. Narrow the topic until you have found a topic that interests you and about which you could write three paragraphs.**

- technology
- entertainment
- fitness
- food

Activity C **Review the topic you chose in Activity B. Use the Topic Checklist on the previous page to make sure it is appropriate. Then gather details about the topic by creating a cluster diagram on a separate sheet of paper.**

> ⭐ When you write a **first draft,** you write complete sentences and paragraphs based on your ideas from the prewriting step. You organize your information and present it in a way that makes sense to your readers.

Your task and purpose will affect how much you need to know about your subject as you draft.

Depending on your subject, you may need to. . .

- do research at a library

- interview people to find out their viewpoints

- spend some time thinking on your own

As you draft, ask yourself these questions. . .

✔ Do I know enough about my subject? If not, how can I find out more?

✔ How will I organize the information I am presenting?

A key part of drafting is deciding on an **organizational pattern.**

Possible Organizational Patterns

- Many times you will present a main idea first and then provide details to support it.

- If you are describing an event or creating a list of instructions, you will probably want to use **chronological order,** or time order, from beginning to end.

- If you are comparing and contrasting two things, you may want to discuss their similarities first and then describe their differences.

Tip

An important part of drafting is figuring out what **background information** *you need to include. Background information helps your audience understand your topic.*

Drafting Tips

✔ DO write a complete beginning, middle, and end.

✔ DO write every idea and thought that comes to mind.

✔ DO add new ideas or notes in the margins.

✔ DON'T feel that you have to start at the beginning. You can write the middle or the end first if those are clearer in your mind.

✔ DON'T worry about correct spelling and grammar. You can fix errors in the editing and proofreading stage.

✔ DON'T try to sound like someone else. Write truthfully and naturally so your style and voice shine through.

✔ DO consider going back to the prewriting stage if your topic is too broad, too narrow, or just not a good fit.

Activity

You're the sports editor of your school newspaper, and a student has written to you asking you to explain what the Heisman Trophy is and why it is important. Use the following notes to draft a paragraph for the paper. (You do not need to use all the information.) Arrange the ideas in a logical order. Write your answer on a separate sheet of paper.

Notes

- Heisman Trophy—each year to outstanding college football player
- Winner voted by U.S. sports broadcasters and writers
- Began in 1935
- Awarded each year
- Usually a quarterback or running back
- Named for John W. Heisman, college coach, director of Downtown Athletic Club of New York City
- Some Heisman winners "big names" in pro football—Roger Staubach (1963), Doug Flutie (1984), Reggie Bush (2005)
- Only primarily defensive player to win: Charles Woodson (1997)

LESSON 3 Revising

> Revising **is probably the most important step in the writing process. Use the six traits of good writing to improve your draft until it says, clearly and smoothly, what you want it to say.**

As you revise, you can change words and phrases, rearrange sentences and paragraphs, and add or remove text.

Six Traits of Good Writing

1. **Ideas and Content** Do all my ideas relate to the topic? Is my topic too narrow or broad?
2. **Organization** Have I written a complete beginning, middle, and end? Do I connect one idea clearly to the next?
3. **Sentence Fluency** Does my writing read smoothly and naturally? Do I use a combination of short and long sentences?
4. **Word Choice** Have I used the best possible words to express my meaning?
5. **Voice** Does my draft sound like me?
6. **Conventions** Have I used correct grammar, spelling, punctuation, and capitalization?

Questions for Revising a Story or Other Narrative

✔ Do I need to use more details to describe a character?
✔ Have I given enough information about the setting—where and when the story takes place?
✔ Do the events flow naturally from one to the next?
✔ Does the dialogue sound natural?

Questions for Revising an Expository Essay

✔ Does my introduction draw the reader in?
✔ Is each paragraph about one main idea?
✔ Do I express my ideas clearly and in a logical order?
✔ Should I do more research so I can better explain certain ideas?

Tip

Reading your work aloud can help you find places that are confusing or that don't sound natural. You can read the work to yourself or to a classmate.

14 *Writers at Work*

Questions for Revising Persuasive Writing

✔ Is what I believe about the issue clear?

✔ Have I considered both sides of the issue?

✔ What opposing arguments might a reader have, and how could I answer them?

Questions for Revising Any Kind of Writing

✔ Have I used the best possible words to express my meaning?

✔ Do all my ideas relate to the topic?

✔ Does my writing read smoothly and naturally?

Model

Add main idea.

Delete unnecessary details.

> ¶To make an overhand serve in volleyball, follow these steps. You must decide which hand you will use to hit the ball. ~~You~~ Use
> ~~should hit the ball with~~ the hand that is stronger and more comfortable for you. ~~Sometimes even left-handed players hit the ball with the right hand.~~

Peer review can be helpful during the revision stage. With a classmate, take turns reading your work aloud. Then discuss the strengths and weaknesses of one another's work and offer respectful suggestions for improvement.

Tips for Peer Reviewing

✔ **Listen carefully.** Jot down your comments while your partner is reading aloud from his or her paper.

✔ **Make positive comments first.** It can be nerve-racking to read your writing to someone else! Be considerate of others' feelings.

✔ **Be specific.** *What* did you like about the introduction? *Why* is the dialogue confusing?

✔ **Find out if the other writer wants you to focus on a specific area.** Some peer reviewers might want help with plot or with word choice. Others are open to comments on all parts of the writing.

✔ **Don't be defensive.** If you act angry or hurt after peers' comments, they won't share their true opinions with you.

Activity A This paragraph was written for a school newspaper. Use what you have learned to revise the paragraph on a separate sheet of paper. You can use the notes below to add information, or you can make up details.

> The Rockvale Middle School Annual Food Drive was a disaster this year. I mean it could have been much better. We collected about half of the amount of food that is usually donated during the drive. I think we should be ashamed of ourselves for a job poorly done!

Notes

- Could have been better planned and organized—more publicity needed

- Could send a written notice to each student or display signs around school

- Maybe list kinds of food needed most—can't accept foods that will go stale

- Idea for improving drive: Prize to the class that donates most food?

- Need information: Who gets the food? Why is the drive important?

Activity B Compare your paragraph to your classmates' revisions. What problems did you find? How did you improve your writing? Use the peer review tips on the previous page as you discuss the changes and improvements you made.

Activity C Choose a writing assignment that you are working on for this class, for another class, or just for yourself. Trade papers with a partner, and review each other's drafts.

Editing and Proofreading

> After revising your work, edit and proofread it.
> Correct mistakes in spelling, punctuation, capitalization,
> and grammar. Create a clean and error-free copy of the
> work—your final draft.

Tech Tip

Use the spell-check feature as you revise. However, computer spell-checkers don't always catch usage mistakes, such as using threw when you meant through. Always proofread your work, and check a dictionary as well.

Edit your work by reading it aloud and thinking of how it works as a whole. Is it logical? Does it flow smoothly? Then think about **conventions,** which means correct spelling, punctuation, grammar, mechanics, and usage.

Proofreading Symbols for Correcting Mistakes

dr. thomas lives in chicago.	Capitalize.
the Doctor	Make lowercase.
for June. Next month,	Start a new paragraph.
didn't even see him	Add.
all of the way too the top	Delete.
Mr Suarez went home.	Add a period.
paper, pencils and erasers	Add a comma.
An alarm sounded everyone ran.	Add a semicolon.
What would say you?	Switch order.
icecream	Add a space.
a base ball cap	Close up space.

The inside back cover of this book also shows proofreading symbols. For capitalization and punctuation rules, see the **Writer's Handbook** at the back of this book. On the next page find an example of how proofreaders use their marks.

The P͟refect Catch

it was the top of the ninth and my team was on the
field the visitors had two outs and we were ahead by won ^one

run. Smack! I saw the ball comeing straight at me. I ran back

with my glove pointed upward then the next thing I saw was

the sky. I musthave tripped over something. I just closed my

eyes and held out my glove. When I herd ^a the cheers, I figured

the ball had landed in my glove. Instead of looking clumsy, I

become ^a the hero of the day!

Activity **Use proofreader's symbols to mark corrections in the paragraph below.**

Along ago, the stars could be both seen at nihgt and day.
Night star were children of the moon day stars were children
of the sun. One day moon told the sun that the children were
trying to outshine both of them. The moon and sun agreed to
put all the stars in the ocean where they could no long shine.
The moon decided not keep her part of the agreement So,
the moon's children stayed in the night sky. The suns children
became multi-colored fish in the ocean. From that time the
sun became the moon's enemy and tried to get revenge for the
deed. When an eclipse occurs, it is because the sun is trying to
eat up the moon.

LESSON 5 Publishing and Presenting

> In the last step of the writing process, you **publish** and **present** your work. In other words, you share your final version with your audience. You may also add your writing to your portfolio.

Many times, you publish your work when you hand in your assignment to your teacher. However, there are a variety of other ways for student writers to publish their work.

Tech Tip

The way you publish your writing may affect how you express yourself. For instance, if you are creating a slide-show presentation, change paragraphs into short, bulleted lists.

Ways to Publish Your Writing

✔ Post an essay, story, or article to a website that your school publishes.

✔ Submit a story, poem, or article to your school's literary magazine.

✔ Enter an essay contest sponsored by a newspaper, magazine, business, website, or other organization.

✔ Submit work to a literary magazine that publishes work by and for young people.

✔ Submit an editorial or article to a newspaper or magazine.

✔ Use presentation software to create a slide show.

✔ Use desktop publishing software to create a brochure.

✔ Turn your writing into a persuasive speech that you can deliver to classmates or community members.

✔ Add video clips, sound clips, posters, graphs, or charts to make a multimedia presentation that showcases your work.

✔ Put your writing on a smartphone.

✔ Become a director! Borrow a video camera, and create a movie or documentary.

✔ Create your own blog or website to share your point of view.

Organize samples of your writing in a **writer's portfolio.** Include finished pieces that you especially like, as well as early drafts of your writing. Your portfolio will show the progress you have made as a writer.

Activity A Get together with a partner. For each item listed below, brainstorm three possible ways to publish or present it. Write your responses on a separate sheet of paper.

1. a fictional description of exploring the planet Mercury

2. an explanation of how to program a cell phone

3. an opinion about a new holiday that should be added to your school's vacation schedule

4. a description of what a marketplace in ancient Rome looked and sounded like

5. an explanation of why your favorite television show should not be canceled

6. a description of how a caterpillar becomes a butterfly

7. your feelings about a recent accomplishment of yours

8. a step-by-step explanation of how to create a podcast

9. childhood memories of playing a favorite game

10. a description of what you did on your summer vacation

Activity B Assemble a portfolio of your writing from this class and from social studies, science, and other classes. Then answer the questions, writing your responses on a separate sheet of paper.

1. Which piece is your favorite? Why?

2. Which piece got the most positive reaction from its audience? Why?

3. Which piece would benefit from revision? How would you revise it?

4. Which piece could you republish in a different format? What format?

Focusing on Word Choice

When you write, you need to choose words that create clear pictures and are grammatically correct. In this lesson, you'll improve your skills at selecting words that say what you mean—precisely and correctly.

LESSON ① Be Precise

> ⭐ **To make your writing clearer, replace vague, general nouns with concrete nouns. Use vivid verbs to make writing lively and exciting and to give your reader a clear picture of the action.**

Use concrete, or specific nouns, to name people, places, things, and ideas:

> **General** Alcina added many *things* to the boiling soup.
>
> **Concrete** Alcina added *salt*, *pepper*, *thyme*, and *basil* to the boiling soup.
>
> **General** The *woman* enjoys watching *shows*.
>
> **Concrete** Mrs. Woo enjoys watching *reality shows*, *documentaries*, and *news programs*.

Tip

Using vivid verbs helps you get to your point quickly, without using lots of adverbs. For instance, you can replace "The dog went quickly and happily to the toy" with "The dog scampered to the toy."

Use vivid verbs to name specific actions:

> **Vague** The guide *made* a trail through the brush.
>
> **Vivid** The guide *hacked* and *stomped* a trail through the brush.
>
> **Vague** The racehorse *walked* across the finish line.
>
> **Vivid** The racehorse *limped* across the finish line.

Activity A On a separate sheet of paper, rewrite each sentence, using a vivid verb to replace each italicized verb. You can add or replace other words to create a sharper picture for the reader.

1. "Can we *go* to the zoo?" I *asked*.

2. The runners *placed* themselves on the starting line.

3. Please *get* that child back to her seat.

4. The silver automobile *went* down the steep hill.

5. The three-stage rocket *moved* from the launch pad.

Activity B In the following paragraph, replace general nouns and verbs with precise ones. (You may add details to make the paragraph more interesting.) Write your changes on a separate sheet of paper.

   Two people went across a field at twilight. There was a ruined house, and they went inside. They stopped in the room. Suddenly, a creature flew around their heads. From the dark stairway came a noise.

Activity C On a separate sheet of paper, write a paragraph about the picture. Use at least five concrete nouns and at least five vivid verbs, underlining each.

Use the Best Descriptive Word

⭐ **Use precise adjectives and adverbs instead of vague or overused ones.**

Have you read a description that helps you imagine being in the scene itself? When choosing a descriptive word, ask yourself if the word is specific enough to create a vivid image.

💬 Tech Tip

Use your computer's Search Text feature to see how many times you use certain adjectives and adverbs. If your reader constantly sees the words amazing *or* totally, *those words start to lose their power.*

Examples of Vague Modifiers

> good, fine, bad, awful, cute, pretty, super, great, very, really

Compare the italicized modifiers in each pair of sentences. Think about how the modifiers in the second sentences help create more specific pictures.

> **Vague** *Very old* leaves cluttered the once *great* park.
>
> **Precise** *Brittle, rotting* leaves cluttered the once *majestic* park.
>
> **Vague** A pigeon flew *badly* toward the *awful* playground.
>
> **Precise** A pigeon flew *awkwardly* toward the *ruined* playground.

Activity A **On a separate sheet of paper, write a descriptive word or phrase that can replace each italicized word to make the sentence more precise. (You can also change other words in the sentence to make your changes read smoothly.)**

1. The ruby-throated hummingbird is a *cute* bird.

2. An unchecked oil spill is *bad* for wildlife.

3. A *good* pilot watches the gauges closely.

Activity A *continued*

4. The final race for the snowy summit was *great*.

5. Kline's new book has a *very neat* cover.

6. You sang *nicely* at the International Festival last weekend.

7. Erina played the character so *well* that we believed she was real.

8. The apartment at the end of Ivy Street was collapsing *awfully badly*.

9. Electricity can provide *super* energy for operating hybrid cars.

10. Guided by ancient artists, Hopi potters today create *pretty* pots.

Activity B

Each sentence has two lettered blanks. For each blank, there is a lettered guide question to help you think of one or more precise modifiers. Write the modifier or modifiers on the blank. One has been done as a sample.

1. The _____(a)_____ train chugged _____(b)_____ along rusted tracks.

   a. How did the train look? *old-fashioned*
   b. How fast did it move? _____

2. A _____(a)_____ girl danced _____(b)_____, even after the music stopped.

   a. How did the girl feel? _____
   b. How was the girl dancing? _____

3. I can see the _____(a)_____ tulips from my _____(b)_____ window.

   a. What color are the tulips? _____
   b. What size is the window? _____

4. A _____(a)_____ mask enhanced the effect of the _____(b)_____ ceremony.

   a. What was the mask like? _____
   b. How old is the ceremony? _____

5. The _____(a)_____ mongrel greeted me _____(b)_____ in the park.

   a. What size was the dog? _____
   b. How happy was the dog to meet someone? _____

Choose the Adjective or the Adverb

⭐ **Use an adjective to describe a noun or a pronoun. Use an adverb to describe a verb, an adjective, or another adverb.**

To figure out whether to use an adjective or an adverb, first identify the word you need to modify.

Examples of Adjectives and Adverbs

>   *adjective*   *adjective*
> Zoe is *quick*. Fred told me that she is a *quick* runner.
>
>   *adverb*   *adverb*   *adverb*
> Zoe runs *quickly*. In fact, she runs *unbelievably quickly*.

Use adjectives after **linking verbs,** which are verbs that don't express action.

> **Common Linking Verbs**
>
> all forms of the verb *to be* (*am, is, are, was, were, been*), *look, appear, feel, taste, smell, sound, stay, seem, become*
>
> **Examples**
>
> She appears *content*. (not *contentedly*)
>
> The cat with black spots looks *hungry*. (not *hungrily*)

Remember that *good* and *bad* are adjectives; *well* and *badly* are adverbs. As an adjective, *well* refers to health.

>   *adjective*   *adjective*
> It's a *good* idea to go running now that you feel *well*.
>
>   *adverb*   *adjective*
> Teresa sang *badly* because she has a *bad* cold.

Tip

Remember that an adverb tells how, when, or where something happened. Many adverbs are formed by adding -ly to an adjective, as in wild *and* wildly.

Activity A **Read each sentence, and circle the correct answer.**

1. Because the road curved ahead, the driver could not see (clear, clearly).

2. You appear (happy, happily) that you won first prize!

3. I will pay you (generous, generously) if you complete the job today.

4. Though he was sick yesterday, he seems quite (good, well) today.

5. I slept (bad, badly) last night and had (bad, badly) dreams.

6. Mario cooks (good, well) and plans to be a chef.

7. This flannel shirt feels so (soft, softly)!

8. Whenever you need help, just call me (quick, quickly).

9. It is (essential, essentially) that our school improve its recycling program.

10. Jalapeños taste too (spicy, spicily) to me.

Activity B **Read each sentence below. If the underlined modifier is correct, put a check mark in front of the sentence. If it is incorrect, write the correct word in the blank.**

_____ 1. She finished her drawing <u>careful</u>.

_____ 2. Shoshi swims <u>good</u>.

_____ 3. If you install antivirus software <u>prompt</u>, you will avoid many computer problems.

_____ 4. The black rock, worn by water, felt <u>smooth</u> to the touch.

_____ 5. Eating <u>good</u> is important for your health.

LESSON ④ Compare Correctly

> ★ When you are comparing two things, use the **comparative** form of the adjective or adverb. To make the comparative form, add *-er* or use the word *more*. When you are comparing more than two things, use the **superlative** form by adding *-est* or using the word *most*.

Examples of the Comparative Form

Add -er to one-syllable words and some two-syllable words.

Add more to some two-syllable words and all three-syllable words.

Roberto wrote a *longer* story than Sierra wrote.

The main character is *braver* and *stronger* than the villain.

Darnell's story is much *more imaginative* than mine.

Examples of the Superlative Form

Carey wrote the *longest* story in our writing club.

That story's hero is the *bravest* and *strongest* of all.

One student will win a hundred-dollar prize for the *most imaginative* short story.

Watch out for some adjectives and adverbs that don't follow these rules. Be careful, too, to avoid double comparisons.

Adjective/Adverb	Comparative	Superlative
good/well	better	best
bad/badly	worse	worst
many/much	more	most
little/less	less	least

Avoiding Double Comparisons

Use *more/most* or
-er/-est but not both.

Incorrect	Lourdes is the *most funniest* joker in our class.
Correct	Lourdes is the *funniest* joker in our class.
Incorrect	I wish I could do *more better* work in Spanish class.
Correct	I wish I could do *better* work in Spanish class.

Activity   Read the main sentences and the accompanying sentences with blanks. Fill in each blank to complete the comparison correctly. The first one has been done.

1. Toni won the 100-meter dash, while Rosa finished third. (fast)

   a. Toni ran ___*faster*___ than Rosa.
   b. Toni was the _____ runner in the race.

2. Sarah is five feet tall; Paul is five feet, five inches; Allie is four feet, eleven inches. (tall, short)

   a. Sarah is _____ than Allie.
   b. Allie is _____ than Paul.
   c. Paul is the _____ person in the group.

3. The announcement for the ceremony said, "Suits and dresses preferred. No jeans or T-shirts, please." (good)

   a. I guess jeans and a T-shirt would not be the _____ choice.
   b. Is a suit _____ to wear than a dress?
   c. My _____ option is my black suit.

4. Mr. Lucas has three pigs on his farm. Clippo is small, Bowtie is big, and Mammoth is so huge that he needs a special door. (big, small)

   a. Mammoth is the _____ pig on that farm.
   b. Bowtie is _____ than Clippo.
   c. Clippo is the _____ of the three.

5. I saved 5 dollars. Jo saved only 2 dollars, but Ben saved 10! (much, less)

   a. Jo saved the _____ amount of money of the three of us.
   b. I saved _____ than Ben but _____ than Jo.

Writing Correct Sentences

When you write complete and correct sentences, your reader can move with ease from one sentence to the next.

LESSON ① Fix Fragments and Run-on Sentences

Tech Tip

A computer's grammar checker will point out fragments. However, grammar checkers are sometimes unreliable, so check your work yourself as well.

> ★ **A fragment is a sentence that is not complete. It may be missing a subject, a predicate, or both.**

A complete sentence has a subject and a predicate, and it expresses a complete thought. The **subject,** which always has at least one noun or pronoun, tells who or what the sentence is about. The **predicate,** which always has at least one verb, tells what the subject is, what it does, or what happens to it.

The subject of an imperative sentence is *you* (understood).

Subjects	Predicates
noun Food *additives*	*verb* sometimes *provide* nutrition.
pronoun They	*verb* *verb* *may* also *add* flavor.
(The understood *you*)	*verb* *Pay* attention to food labels.

To fix a fragment, add the missing part.

If you ask, "Who or what is this about?" add a subject.

> **Fragment** Decided to open a shop.
>
> **Complete Sentence** *Luis and Al* decided to open a shop.

If you ask, "What about it?" add a predicate.

Fragment Third Avenue, with its many small shops.

Complete Sentence Third Avenue, with its many small shops, *was already crowded with businesses.*

⭐ A **run-on sentence** contains two or more complete sentences run together without proper punctuation.

In some run-on sentences, the writer puts two complete sentences together without separating the sentences with any punctuation.

The Great Barrier Reef of Australia is the world's largest reef it is formed by hundreds of species of coral.

In others, the writer separates the sentences with only a comma.

Coral has two cell layers, one layer is called the ectoderm, while the other layer is called the endoderm.

Four Ways to Fix a Run-on Sentence

Make Two Sentences The Great Barrier Reef of Australia is the world's largest reef. *It* is formed by hundreds of species of coral.

Rewrite It as a Compound Sentence The Great Barrier Reef of Australia is the world's largest reef, *and it* is formed by hundreds of species of coral.

Separate It with a Semicolon The Great Barrier Reef of Australia is the world's largest reef; *it* is formed by hundreds of species of coral.

Rewrite It as a Sentence with a Subordinate Clause The Great Barrier Reef of Australia, *which is formed by hundreds of species of coral,* is the world's largest reef.

Activity A Label each item as a sentence (S) or a fragment (F).
On a separate sheet of paper, correct each fragment.

____ **1.** Listening to the sound of beeping horns.

____ **2.** The guests arrived.

____ **3.** Several of the most talkative students.

____ **4.** Buzzed annoyingly.

____ **5.** The sad-looking young woman at the subway station.

____ **6.** Don't forget to place the order for the sneakers.

____ **7.** Forgot to place the order for the sneakers.

____ **8.** Due to the very heavy rains of last September.

____ **9.** Please quiet down.

____ **10.** Accidentally cornered Tasha's cat on the stairs.

Activity B Fix the fragments and run-on sentences in this e-mail.
Copy the corrected message on a separate piece of paper.

I bought a pair of your Fleet Feet sneakers two months ago. Model number 682, size 7. Playing a lot of tennis, a hole in the sole of right shoe just under my big toe. I am very unhappy about this hole. Because the sneakers cost $99. Should last more than two months. Please give me the address where I can send them for repairs, if you can't repair them promptly please send a replacement pair. I need these sneakers right away, tournament coming up in two weeks! Thanks for your help.

Make Subjects and Verbs Agree

> ★ If the subject of a sentence is singular, you must use a singular verb. If the subject of a sentence is plural, you must use a plural verb.

The subject of a sentence (the "who" or "what") can be singular or plural. A **singular subject** names only one person or thing. A **plural subject** names more than one person or thing.

Most singular verbs have an -s ending. Most plural verbs don't.

> **Singular Verbs** The boy *practices*. She *draws*. The jacket *fits*.
>
> **Plural Verbs** The boys *practice*. We *draw*. The shoes *fit*.

Three verbs—*be*, *have*, and *do*—have special forms.

Tip

If the subject is a single thing, it takes a singular verb, even if the subject contains more than one noun: Peanut butter and jelly is my favorite sandwich.

Singular Subject	Present-Tense Verb	Past-Tense Verb
I	am, have, do	was, had, did
you	are, have, do	were, had, did
he, she, it, or singular noun	is, has, does	was, had, did
Plural Subject	**Present-Tense Verb**	**Past-Tense Verb**
we, you, they, or plural noun	are, have, do	were, had, did

Sometimes you have to read a sentence carefully to determine if the subject is singular or plural. Study the examples on the next page.

Words Separating Subject and Verb

A verb never agrees with any word in an interrupting phrase or clause.

The *dresses* that we looked at in the department store *were* well made.

The *uniforms* for the girls' basketball team *are* finally on their way.

Subjects Joined by *And*

Use a plural verb when two singular subjects are joined by *and*.

Antonio and *David* always *lead* the football team onto the field a few minutes before the game starts.

Michael and *Maria* are the most talented musicians in the entire school.

Two or More Subjects Joined by *Or* or *Nor*

The verb agrees with the subject that is next to it.

Either the *coaches* or *David leads* the football team onto the field a few minutes before the game starts.

Surprisingly, neither *Rose* nor *Travis wants* to run for class president this year.

Tip

These subjects always take a singular verb:
each   one
either   everybody
neither   anyone

Words That Refer to a Single Person or Group

Each of the girls *contributes* to St. Scholastica Academy's soccer team in a different way.

Neither of the girls *wants* to quit the team in the middle of the season.

Everybody agrees that both girls are important to the team and deserve a special award.

Activity Cross out each incorrect verb, and write the correct verb form above it. Before you begin, review the rules for subject-verb agreement on the first two pages of this lesson. (Hint: You should find six mistakes in this passage.)

Last week our class and Ms. Lu's class was studying endangered species, and now everyone in our class are writing a report. Each of our reports is supposed to include drawings or maps. Either Sonia or Luis are writing about the passenger pigeon. Passenger pigeons, great auks, and dusky sparrows are among the extinct species. Now each of those species are gone forever. Jeff and I are writing about sea turtles.

Environmentalists and concerned citizens ask Congress for laws to protect endangered species, but many people in our region of the country disagrees strongly with such legislation. Laws protecting the spotted owl, for example, has disrupted the lumber industry in the Pacific Northwest and endangered jobs and businesses in Washington and Oregon.

spotted owl

Use the Right Verb Form

> ⭐ Both regular and irregular verbs have different forms, or principal parts. The three forms you will use often in your writing are the present, the past, and the past participle.

Present	Past	Past Participle
dance	danced	(had) danced
mix	mixed	(had) mixed
ruin	ruined	(had) ruined

The present describes actions that are happening now. The past shows an action that has already happened. To form the past of a regular verb, add *-d* or *-ed*.

To form the past participle of a regular verb, add *-d* or *-ed* and use *has*, *had*, or *have*.

Some verbs do not use the *-ed* ending to form the past tense and past participle. These irregular verbs don't follow any rule.

Irregular Verb Forms

Present	Past	Past Participle (used with *has*, *have*, or *had*)
be (am, is, are)	was, were	been
begin	began	begun
break	broke	broken
bring	brought	brought
catch	caught	caught
do (do, does)	did	done
give	gave	given

Irregular Verb Forms (continued)

Verb	Past	Past Participle (used with *has*, *have*, or *had*)
go	went	gone
have (has, have)	had	had
lose	lost	lost
lie	lay	lain
rise	rose	risen
take	took	taken
wear	wore	worn

Activity Each sentence below contains an incorrect verb form. Write the correct verb form on the line.

_____ **1.** We watched until the geese *soar* out of sight.

_____ **2.** What *has* Patricia *weared* over her costume?

_____ **3.** The dinosaur bone *breaked* with a crunch.

_____ **4.** Jay expertly *catched* the wriggling trout.

_____ **5.** After dinner, Leah *complete* her homework.

_____ **6.** I *brang* the music to the party.

_____ **7.** Your dog *begun* to bark at the taxi.

_____ **8.** Yesterday Bridget *taken* her baby sister to the park.

_____ **9.** The queen *has rule* her country wisely for ten years.

_____ **10.** My grandmother *have* birdhouses in her backyard.

Making Sentences Clear and Lively

If your sentences all sound the same, your reader is likely to become bored. If your sentences are wordy, your reader is likely to become confused. A well-written piece has a variety of sentences that flow smoothly together and clearly communicate meaning.

LESSON 1 Combine Ideas

> ⭐ **Combining sentences that have related ideas makes your writing smoother and more sophisticated. Use conjunctions, clauses, and pronouns to put sentences together.**

Read these sentences, and think about how they sound.

> You can help prevent tooth decay. You can drink fluoridated water. You can use toothpaste with fluoride to prevent tooth decay. You can also get fluoride treatments. You can ask your dentist to give you fluoride treatments at the dentist to help prevent tooth decay.

Are the sentences pleasing, or do they sound choppy, repetitive, and immature? Combining the sentences makes the writing sound more appealing and sophisticated.

> To help prevent tooth decay, you can drink fluoridated water, use toothpaste with fluoride, and ask your dentist for fluoride treatments.

The **coordinating conjunction** *and* tells how the ideas are linked. Add a comma before a coordinating conjunction.

> **Separate** I attend a language class after school. That time of day is also when I play soccer. I also roller-skate after school.
>
> **Combined** I attend a language class, play soccer, *and* roller-skate after school.

You can combine some sentences by forming a main clause and a subordinate clause. The **main clause** expresses the more important idea. The **subordinate clause** is attached to the main clause and cannot stand on its own as a complete sentence.

> **Separate** We get water in our basement. It happens whenever it rains.
>
> *subordinate clause*   *main clause*
>
> **Combined** *Whenever it rains,* we get water in our basement.

Words such as *whenever, although, because, since,* and *until* are **subordinating conjunctions** that you can use to combine sentences.

> **Separate** Rachel Carson believed in protecting the environment. She wrote books to inform others.
>
> **Combined** *Because* she believed in protecting the environment, Rachel Carson wrote books to inform others.

Words such as *who, which, what,* and *that* are **relative pronouns** that you can use to combine sentences.

> **Separate** Theresa is a good student. She likes to play basketball.
>
> **Combined** Theresa is a good student *who* likes to play basketball.

Activity A On a separate piece of paper, revise each of the following groups of sentences to make them sound more interesting and less choppy. Make one or two sentences. Combine ideas, delete words, add words, and change word order if you wish.

1. Sign language is different from spoken language. Sign language is visual, not oral. This kind of language is complex. Sign language can take years to learn.

2. I have a website. It is new. My website is fantastic. My website has graphics. They are incredible. I created the graphics myself. My website is easy to navigate. It is filled with useful information.

3. The Maya existed long ago. The Maya existed before Europeans reached the Americas. The Maya had a culture. It was an advanced culture. The Maya had a calendar. The Maya also had a system of writing.

4. Carnivals occur in many South American countries. Carnival is held yearly in Brazil. Carnivals are held yearly on many Caribbean islands. New Orleans has a carnival every year. New Orleans is in North America.

5. A bus drove up our street. The bus was huge. The bus was crowded with children. The children were laughing. The children were screaming. The bus was dusty brown.

Activity B Get together with a small group and exchange the answers you wrote for Activity A. Use this checklist to evaluate your and your classmates' answers.

✔ How did combining sentences improve the quality of the writing?

✔ Did your answers differ? If so, how?

✔ Were any of the combined sentences so long that they became confusing? If so, how would you fix them?

> **Make your sentences concise, or to the point, by deleting unnecessary words.**

In Lesson 1, you learned that you can make your sentences concise by combining ideas. Another way to get to the point quickly is to eliminate repeated words.

> If your assignment has a specific word count, use your computer's word count feature. However, don't add meaningless extra words to reach the assigned number. Instead, spend more time researching or thinking about your topic so your writing has more substance.

Wordy For many centuries before the Spanish *conquistadores* arrived in Mexico ~~from Spain,~~ native Mexican peoples created ~~many kinds of~~ artistic works, ~~and those works were~~ made of ceramics. ~~They were also made of~~ gold and silver. ~~The conquistadores arrived in Mexico in~~ 1519.

Concise For centuries before 1519, when the Spanish *conquistadores* arrived in Mexico, native Mexican peoples created art made of ceramics, gold, and silver.

Watch out for extra *and*'s and other "padding," or meaningless words that can make your writing sound unclear.

Wordy ~~After that,~~ the Spaniards introduced the potter's wheel to the Mexicans, ~~and with the potter's wheel,~~ artists were able to produce large quantities of ceramic plates and ~~also~~ bowls ~~as well.~~

Concise The Spaniards introduced the potter's wheel to the Mexicans, which allowed artists to produce large quantities of ceramic plates and bowls.

Concise writing also makes "real world" writing, such as directions, instructions, and e-mails, more interesting to read and easier to understand.

Activity   Look for unnecessary words in the sentences below. On the lines, revise the sentences to express the same ideas clearly and concisely. You may write more than one sentence.

1.   Collect all the materials you will need before you begin a project. This rule applies to any kind of project. The reason is that you cannot begin until you have everything you need. Otherwise, you may have to stop and gather more materials just when you don't want to stop and go hunting for something.

_____

_____

2.   For several weeks Len has been going to a tae kwon do school where he is learning tae kwon do. Tae kwon do is one of the martial arts, and it is a martial art that comes from Korea. According to Len's instructor, tae kwon do will teach Len confidence. It also teaches him discipline. It will make him physically fit.

_____

_____

3.   If it is possible for a reporter to do it, a reporter should interview an eyewitness who was on the scene whenever the reporter writes a report about an event or a story about an event.

_____

_____

4.   There are two important reasons not to depend totally upon a spell-checking system on a computer for the correct spelling of words. One of the reasons is that a word can be spelled correctly even though it is not the word the writer means. Another of the reasons is because spell-checking systems are not complete.

_____

_____

Vary Sentence Beginnings

> ⭐ **When too many of your sentences begin the same way, your writing sounds repetitive and clumsy. Varying your sentence beginnings makes your writing smoother and more appealing.**

Read this excerpt from a student's story. Which version is livelier?

Notice how many sentences in the first draft begin with a subject followed immediately by a verb. Joining many sentences with the word and *also makes the writing dull.*

First Draft I wanted a pet. I discussed pets with my parents. My first choice was an alligator. My parents said no. My second choice was a lizard, and they said no, and I asked for a snake, and they said no, and I asked for a rat. They said no. I pleaded for a bird, and my parents said yes, so I bought one. The bird was a chicken, and my parents were not too pleased, and they said I had not listened to them. They were wrong.

Revision Wanting a pet, I sat down to talk with my parents. "I'd really love a pet alligator," I suggested. Firmly, my parents responded with a *no*. In turn, I asked for a lizard, a snake, and a rat. *No* was the unshakable response to each animal. So I begged for a bird, and my parents approved. However, when I walked into our house with the chicken I had bought, my parents were upset. They said I had not listened to them, but they were wrong.

Try adding **vivid details** to your sentence beginnings.

First Draft The cat pounced on the mouse.

With Adverbs *Quickly and silently*, the cat pounced on the mouse.

With a Prepositional Phrase *In the inky darkness*, the cat pounced on the mouse.

 **Tech Tip**

Don't forget to vary sentence beginnings in blog entries, e-mails, and personal messages as well as in school assignments.

Adding **phrases** or **clauses** can also help you to vary sentence beginnings.

> **Phrase** *Surprising the mouse*, the cat pounced.
>
> **Phrase** *To surprise the mouse*, the cat pounced.
>
> **Clause** *When the cat pounced in the dark*, the mouse was surprised.

Activity **Revise each sentence, changing its beginning. You may combine sentences and eliminate words. Write your answers on a separate sheet of paper.**

1. We sat bundled up in coats and mittens to stay warm.

2. I doubted the bus would ever come, and my breath formed clouds in the chilly air.

3. Ramón won the race at the last minute, and he won it by sprinting ahead.

4. The shooting star blazed brightly along the horizon.

5. The dog raced unexpectedly into the busy intersection.

6. Emily gave up fishing, and she gave it up after she nearly fell into the lake.

7. The haunting trombone moaned softly and blended its sound with the wind.

8. The trees in the park were dropping their needles noiselessly.

9. The dented, empty garbage cans clanked, and they banged against the wall at midnight.

10. I like eating crunchy apples, and I enjoy sweet peaches, and I also like tangy berries to satisfy my hunger.

Writing Effective Paragraphs

A paragraph should focus on one main idea. If you want to tell about a different idea, start a new paragraph. In this chapter, you will learn how to organize and improve the paragraphs you write.

LESSON ① Write a Topic Sentence

 A **topic sentence** tells the reader the main idea, or overall point, you will focus on in your paragraph.

A **topic sentence** usually appears at the beginning of a paragraph. You can, however, put your topic sentence at the end or even in the middle of a paragraph, as long as your ideas flow smoothly.

A good topic sentence. . .

✔ tells readers what the paragraph is about
✔ expresses the main idea you want to make about the subject
✔ makes the reader want to keep reading

Example

> Air bags may add to the cost of a car or truck, but they are one of the most important safety features available in vehicles today.

This topic sentence introduces the paragraph's subject and raises questions that the reader expects the paragraph to explain. How do air bags protect drivers and passengers? How expensive are they? Why are other available safety features not as important?

Activity A

After reading each paragraph, choose the best topic sentence for the paragraph. Circle the letter of that sentence. Then write a reason for your choice on the lines below.

1.   This folklore is expressed in the celebration of the Chinese New Year. During the first seven days, the birthdays of various plants and animals are observed. The seventh day of this celebration is known as the Birthday of Humankind. According to tradition, good weather on this day means that plants and animals born during the new year will be healthy and prosperous. Bad weather means misfortune for the year.

   a. Chinese folklore shows a deep connection with nature—plants, animals, humans, and even weather conditions.

   b. Folklore includes traditional beliefs, stories, and practices.

   c. The Chinese New Year takes place sometime between January 10 and February 19.

_____

_____

_____

2.   Suppose your office is in Paris, Maine, and you want to call Paris, France. You had better make the call early, because if it's 9:00 A.M. in Maine, it's 3:00 P.M. in France. If you work in Melbourne, Australia, and have to call Melbourne, Florida, you may have a problem. As you leave your Australian office at 5:00 P.M., most people in Florida are sleeping. After all, it is only 2:00 A.M. in the Sunshine State.

   a. The currently accepted system of world time zones includes twenty-four zones.

   b. Be aware of time zones if your job requires you to make phone calls to other countries.

   c. The continental United States has four time zones.

_____

_____

_____

Activity B   Read each group of sentences below. On the lines above them, write a topic sentence that could introduce the paragraph well. (Write a complete sentence, not a title.)

1. Topic Sentence: _____

_____

_____

At the beginning of the Revolution, the Continental Army carried smallpox all through the colonies. General Washington ordered a mass inoculation. In the 1700s, doctors inoculated people by exposing them to a mild form of smallpox while they were healthy. This prevented them from getting sick with the deadly form of the disease. In the late 1700s, nearly ten thousand residents were inoculated when smallpox threatened Boston. By 1800, Americans had this disease well under control.

2. Topic Sentence: _____

_____

_____

First of all, the invention of baseball should not be credited exclusively to the United States. Most likely, baseball was derived from the British game of cricket. In addition, Cuba, Puerto Rico, and Mexico have major- and minor-league baseball teams. One of the most popular sports in Japan is baseball.

3. Topic Sentence: _____

_____

_____

Planning and hard work come easily to me. The more complicated the task, the more I like it. I set high standards for myself, and I always try to do more than others expect from me.

LESSON ② Organize Ideas

> To make your ideas clear, begin your paragraph with a **topic sentence**, and then provide details in **chronological order** or in **spatial order**.

When your purpose is to write instructions or describe a process, it is important to make sure all details are in order. First, write a topic sentence so your reader knows what you are describing. Then list steps in the order they occur—**chronological order,** also called time order.

Example of Chronological Order

Chicken tacos are easy to make. To begin, gather the necessary ingredients: taco shells, taco seasoning mix, water, boneless chicken breasts, cheese, tomatoes, lettuce, and whatever other vegetables you want. Next, grate the cheese, shred the lettuce, and chop the remaining vegetables into small pieces. Cut the chicken into bite-sized pieces. Put a thin layer of oil in a frying pan, and thoroughly brown the chicken. Then follow the instructions on the seasoning-mix package to make the sauce, and add the chicken to the heated sauce. Now, place an oven-warmed taco shell on your plate, and pile on the ingredients. Finally, eat your creation!

If the steps in the process were out of order, it would be difficult or impossible to follow these instructions.

When you are describing a scene, you may want to use **spatial order.** In other words, you describe a scene in a logical order from one part to the other.

Types of spatial order include. . .

✔ from left to right (or from right to left)
✔ from top to bottom (or from bottom to top)
✔ from inside to outside (or from outside to inside)
✔ from far away to up close (or from up close to far away)

 **Tech Tip**

If you are not sure of the direction you want your writing to take, use the computer's Save As feature to create different versions of your document.

Example of Spatial Order

> Luis couldn't wait to have dinner. In the brightly lit hallway outside the apartment, he could smell his mother's special *arroz con pollo,* rice with chicken. He turned his key, pushed open the heavy brown door, and stepped inside into warm air filled with the scent of spices, tomatoes, garlic, and onions. He knew that further inside, in the kitchen, the tasty chicken and rice simmered in the black iron pot on the stove.

Include **transition words** that signal to your reader how you are organizing your writing.

Examples of Transition Words

> **For Chronological Order** *to begin, first, second, third, then, next, after that, meanwhile, now, finally, at the end*
>
> **For Spatial Order** *outside, inside, further inside, in the center, on the left, on the right, on the edges, near, far, closer, farther away, at the top, at the bottom*

Activity A **Refer to the example paragraph on the first page of this lesson to answer each question.**

1. What is the topic sentence of the paragraph? Circle it.

2. Where does the writer name the ingredients? Underline them.

3. What transition words can you find in the paragraph? List them on the lines below.

_____

_____

Activity B **Refer to the example paragraph that begins with "Luis couldn't wait to have dinner." Then answer each question.**

1. What is the topic sentence of the paragraph? Circle it.

2. What type of spatial order does the writer use?

_____

3. What transition words can you find in the paragraph? List them.

_____

_____

For each topic, identify the type of order you would use. Write the type of order, and explain why you chose it. Your answers should be complete sentences.

1. how to troubleshoot a common computer problem _____

_____

2. your morning routine before you leave for school _____

_____

3. what your room looks like _____

_____

4. your favorite family photograph _____

_____

Activity D **Choose a topic listed in Activity C. On a separate sheet of paper, write a paragraph of at least five sentences describing the topic. Use chronological or spatial order. Include at least three transitions.**

⭐ **Elaborating** means providing enough details and examples to give your reader a clear understanding of your subject.

Read the following draft of a paragraph that does not give enough information.

> In 1947, a sculptor accepted an invitation to create the largest sculpture in the world. The sculpture was planned to be a tribute to all Native Americans. Because he knew this project could not be completed in any person's lifetime, the sculptor wrote books with plans for the carving.

This paragraph makes the reader ask. . .

- Who was the sculptor?
- Who offered the invitation?
- What would the sculpture show, how large would it be, and where would it be located?

Here is how the writer revised her explanation of this project.

> In 1947, sculptor Korczak Ziolkowski accepted an invitation from Native American leaders to create the largest sculpture in the world—563 feet high and 641 feet long. The sculpture, which would be carved out of a mountain in South Dakota, would be a tribute to all Native American peoples. The monument would be of Crazy Horse, the famous chief of the Lakota. Crazy Horse dedicated his life to defending his people's right to live freely, away from government reservations. Because Ziolkowski knew this project could not be completed in any person's lifetime, he wrote three books with detailed plans for the carving.

When you revise your writing, add information to make your paragraph clearer and more convincing.

Tell your reader more by elaborating with. . .

✔ facts: things that can be proven true
✔ examples: things that illustrate a point
✔ reasons: causes of or explanations of why something occurred
✔ statistics: specific numbers, such as amount or percentage
✔ dates: specific times when events occurred

Activity A **You are a reporter at a weekly news magazine. Review these paragraphs, which will appear in next week's edition. Add support for each paragraph by writing one more sentence. Make up details.**

1. The blizzard caused an almost total shutdown of the Northeast. Airports were closed from Baltimore, Maryland, to Bangor, Maine. Most retail stores were unable to open because roads were blocked.

_____

_____

2. People no longer have to travel the world to eat international foods. In many homes, Italian pasta and sauces are served regularly. Mexican and Tex-Mex restaurants offer tortillas, tacos, enchiladas, and guacamole.

_____

_____

3. Frustrated students often mistakenly think the math skills they are forced to learn will not be useful in the future. However, accountants could give several reasons for becoming skilled in basic math. Without knowledge of fractions, carpenters would not be able to build a house.

_____

_____

Activity B **You are the editor-in-chief of your school newspaper. Your classmates have suggested these topics for the next issue. For each item, write three questions that will encourage the reporter to add supporting details. (Hint: Ask questions using the words *who, what, where, when, why,* and *how.*)**

1. Our grade will have a special assembly soon.

2. There is going to be a dance.

3. The principal announced that school lunches will change.

4. The newly remodeled gym has many features.

5. Next year the school day will begin later.

6. It would be a good idea to have more vending machines.

7. The fund-raiser made lots of money.

8. Construction near the school will cause problems.

9. The Spanish Club is taking a trip.

10. The Parent-Teacher-Student Association will meet.

Activity C **Read each sentence below. Revise each sentence so it is extremely exaggerated. On a separate sheet of paper, write at least one sentence for each answer. One has been done as a sample.**

1. It was a rather large dog. *It was the biggest, hairiest dog I had ever seen—and it wanted to be my friend.*

2. My first evening of babysitting didn't go very well.

3. My grandfather cooked us a big breakfast.

4. In only four days, I learned to roller-skate.

LESSON ④ Unify Your Paragraph

> ⭐ **In a unified paragraph,** all the sentences should relate to one another and support the topic sentence.

Read the paragraph below, which is from a student's science report. The first sentence of the paragraph is the main idea. Which of the other sentences does not tell about the main idea?

> Waves are created by different sources and travel through different substances. Earthquake waves cause tremors in Earth's surface. Televisions and remote control units release electromagnetic waves. Some kitchen ovens use microwaves to heat food. Wood stoves give off powerful heat waves. Surfers measure ocean waves to determine whether it is safe to surf that day.

The last sentence describes why surfers measure waves. This idea does not support the main idea that different sources create waves in different substances. Therefore, the last sentence does not belong in this paragraph.

 **Tech Tip**

If you are writing on a computer, you don't need to use the ¶ symbol. Just move your cursor to wherever you want to begin a new paragraph, and then hit the Return key.

Questions to Improve Unity

✔ What is the topic sentence of the paragraph?

✔ Does every sentence in the paragraph provide important information about the topic sentence?

✔ If a sentence does not belong in this paragraph, should I delete it, or should I make it part of a new paragraph?

If you think one paragraph should be broken into two, place the proofreader's symbol ¶ before the sentence that starts the second paragraph. Be careful, however, that each paragraph is developed enough. Most paragraphs need at least three sentences.

Activity A   **Each paragraph below begins with a topic sentence. On the lines, write the letter of the sentence that does not support the topic, and give a brief reason.**

1.   Doctors use antibiotics to treat infections. (a) Antibiotics contain chemicals produced by microscopic plants or animals. (b) These chemicals kill other microscopic plants and animals that are causing the infection. (c) My cousin Sheila is allergic to the antibiotic penicillin.

Delete sentence _____ because _____

_____

2.   Developing discipline is an important benefit of learning a martial art. (a) A white belt usually indicates a beginner; a black belt indicates an expert. (b) Although many people begin lessons for self-defense, they soon discover the importance of mental and physical concentration. (c) Students learn to control precisely their muscles and movements.

Delete sentence _____ because _____

_____

3.   Olga found the airport scary. (a) Landing and departing planes roared deafeningly. (b) In long lines, people bumped and jostled. (c) The flower shop offered colorful bouquets. (d) A guard snarled, "Hurry!"

Delete sentence _____ because _____

_____

4.   In Western and Eastern cultures, the dragon looks similar but acts differently. (a) In Western myth, the dragon is often an evil force. (b) The dragon of Eastern origin, though frightening in appearance, is a symbol of the creativity and energy of life. (c) I don't like dragons that howl and breathe fire!

Delete sentence _____ because _____

_____

Activity B You are the editor of a travel magazine. Each of the paragraphs below should really be two paragraphs. Use the proofreader's symbol ¶ to show where the second paragraph should begin. Write a brief explanation of your decision on the lines.

1.   During the mid-1400s, the Aztec people of what is now Mexico lived in a complex and structured society. The society was divided into social classes, including nobles, merchants, farmers, and slaves. Each person had a distinct and well-defined role. The Aztec court system was complicated and powerful. In each town, judges handled minor disputes, attempting to keep their claims out of higher courts. The emperor was the Supreme Justice, resolving any disputes not settled in the lower courts. The Aztec also had special courts to meet the needs of merchants and military leaders.

Reason: _____

_____

_____

2.   Consumers are losing millions of dollars every year to fake travel organizations. These phony companies make the same promises as real travel agents: fabulous destinations, convenient flights, and luxurious accommodations—all at low prices. The problem lies in the delivery. Once you give them your money, you never hear from them again. This means you never get to go on the vacation you paid for. How can you spot phony travel claims? Always be careful of an organization that will not give you complete details until receiving your payment or credit card number. Thoroughly check offers that claim you have been selected to receive a fabulous "free" vacation. Be wary of offers that require you to call a 900 number for further information. Most important, use common sense. If someone offers you a deal that sounds too good to be true, it probably is!

Reason: _____

_____

_____

Chapter 6

WORKSHOP

Writing a Compare-Contrast Essay

You've already learned how to create effective paragraphs. Now it's time to use that skill to create something more sophisticated: an essay. An essay is a piece of nonfiction, usually short, that shares information or expresses an opinion. In this chapter, you will write an essay to explain how two things, places, or people are alike (**compare**) and how they are different (**contrast**).

LESSON ❶ Write an Introduction

⭐ **Your introduction tells your reader what you are comparing and contrasting and includes your thesis statement (your main idea). Your introduction should capture your audience's attention.**

Tip

Make sure your thesis is neither too broad nor too narrow.

Too broad: The United States and Canada have many similarities and differences.

Too narrow: Canada and the United States celebrate Thanksgiving on different days.

A good introduction to a compare-contrast essay. . .

✔ names your two subjects of comparison

✔ includes your thesis, which is the main idea of the essay

✔ presents a brief story, an example, a description, a question, or a startling fact that makes your reader want to keep reading

First, know your topic. Your teacher may assign you one or allow you to choose. Your topic should involve two subjects that you know well and that have obvious similarities and differences. An original topic will hold your interest and your reader's interest.

Examples of Compare-Contrast Topics

- two places you have lived in (or visited)
- your two favorite restaurants
- your favorite sport and your least favorite sport

- two types of music (or movies or video games)
- two famous (or infamous) historical figures

Here are some different ways you can structure your introduction. In each example, the thesis statement is highlighted. Notice how each writer uses different techniques to draw the reader in.

Ask a Question

The question and additional details lead into the thesis statement.

Can you imagine playing a video game that has no music, no fancy animation, and hardly any graphics—only two straight lines (for paddles) and a tiny square (for a ball)? Allan Alcorn and Nolan Bushnell invented this game, called Pong, back in 1972. It was an immediate success. Video games have changed tremendously since the 1970s, but today's flashy games are still designed to wow fans and attract new players.

Give a Startling Fact

The thesis names the two subjects being contrasted—artificial turf and natural turf.

The use of artificial turf instead of real turf is ruining professional soccer. While artificial grass is less expensive and easier to take care of than real, natural grass, few fans know that it leads to serious joint injuries that can destroy a player's career. Each year, more players are hurt as soccer stadiums make the switch to artifical turf.

Paint a Word Picture

Vivid descriptions help the reader understand and care about the two subjects.

Imagine taxis honking their horns, neon signs blinking, dozens of fancy stores, and thousands of people crowded onto wide sidewalks. That's what I see when I visit my older sister in the city. Now picture a calm lake next to whispering trees. That's what I see when I go to my aunt's house in the country. My two favorite places to vacation couldn't be more different, but I love them both.

Experiment with different ways of writing your introduction. If you can't think of significant differences between your two topics, choose new topics.

Activity A   Choose two subjects to compare and contrast. On a separate sheet of paper, create a Venn diagram like the one below. On the left and right sides, write the differences between the subjects. In the center, write similarities that they share.

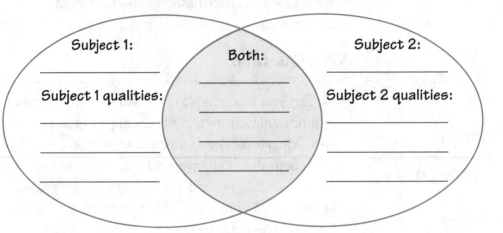

Subject 1: _____

Subject 1 qualities:

_____

_____

_____

Both:

_____

_____

_____

_____

Subject 2: _____

Subject 2 qualities:

_____

_____

_____

Activity B   On a separate sheet of paper, write a thesis and an introductory paragraph based on your notes from Activity A. Make your introduction appealing by including at least one of the following:

- a vivid description
- a question
- a startling fact
- an anecdote
- an example

Activity C   Get together with a classmate, and exchange the paragraphs you wrote for Activity B. Review each other's work. Give specific suggestions to your partner, and listen to his or her comments and opinions. Use these questions as a guide.

✔ How clearly did I state the subjects I am comparing and contrasting?

✔ How effective is my thesis statement?

✔ Does my introductory paragraph make you want to keep reading? If not, what changes would you suggest?

Tip

Try creating an informal outline the next time you answer an essay question on a test. Spend two or three minutes creating a cluster diagram, a flow chart, or another graphic organizer to jot down your ideas.

⭐ A formal or informal outline can help you organize the body of your compare-contrast essay. You can present your ideas using the block method or the point-by-point method.

An **outline** is an organized list of information. The example below shows an outline that uses the **block method.** This student wrote about her first subject (1970s video games) and all the features about it. Then she wrote about her second subject (today's video games).

Block Method Organization

Thesis: Video games have changed tremendously since the 1970s, but today's flashy games are still designed to wow fans and attract new players.

The first subject is labeled with Roman numeral I. The second is Roman numeral II.

I. 1970s games
  A. Game quality
    1. Basic graphics, a few repetitive sound effects
    2. Games had few differences in levels of play
  B. Size
    1. Large and bulky
    2. Home versions not available
  C. Popularity
    1. Very popular
    2. New technology got attention

Notice the indenting for each new piece of information.

II. Today's games
  A. Game quality
    1. Sophisticated graphics, stereo sound
    2. Nearly all games have multiple levels of play
  B. Size
    1. Small, often portable
    2. Home versions available
  C. Popularity
    1. Very popular
    2. New technology gets attention

When you use the **point-by-point method,** you compare or contrast one feature of both topics. Then you compare or contrast a second feature of both topics, and so on.

Point-by-Point Organization

Thesis: Video games have changed tremendously since the 1970s, but today's flashy games are still designed to wow fans and attract new players.

I. Game quality
   A. 1970s video games
      1. Basic graphics, a few repetitive sound effects
      2. Games had few differences in levels of play
   B. Today's games
      1. Sophisticated graphics, stereo sound
      2. Nearly all games have multiple levels of play

II. Size
   A. 1970s games
      1. Large and bulky
      2. Home versions not available
   B. Today's games
      1. Small, often portable
      2. Home versions available

III. Popularity
   A. 1970s games
      1. Very popular
      2. New technology got attention
   B. Today's games
      1. Very popular
      2. New technology gets attention

In a formal outline, if you include a point A, you must include a point B. If you include a point 1, you must include a point 2.

Use your outline to write the **body** of your essay—the middle paragraphs.

Tips for Writing Body Paragraphs

✔ Expand on and explain each fact you included in your outline.

✔ Write approximately the same amount of text for each point.

✔ Don't wander away from your main points. If you want to add new information, revise your outline.

As you write the body paragraphs of your essay, use **transitions.** These help your reader understand how your ideas connect to each other.

Transitions That Show Comparisons

> similarly, like, in the same way, has in common

Transitions That Show Contrasts

> differently, unlike, in sharp contrast, on the other hand

Transitions That Show Sequence

> first, next, then, after that, at the same time, in the past, in 2004, in 2008, in the future

Activity A **Complete the statements below. Then, on a separate sheet of paper, create an outline to organize your compare-contrast essay. Next, write a draft of the body paragraphs of your essay.**

I will write about _____ and _____.

I will use the _____ method of organization.

Activity B **Exchange papers with a classmate. Review each other's outlines and body paragraphs. Give specific suggestions to your partner, and listen to his or her comments and opinions.**

> ★ End your essay with a **conclusion** that makes your reader think again about the thesis. Your conclusion should tie together or summarize the details you presented in the essay.

💻 Tech Tip

Consider turning your compare-contrast essay into a slide-show presentation. If you wish, add photographs, video clips, or animation that helps your audience understand your main points.

A good conclusion to a compare-contrast essay. . .

✔ is one paragraph long

✔ restates the main points you made but uses fresh, new language instead of repeating earlier words and phrases

✔ leaves readers with a final thought about your subject

How you conclude your essay depends on what you have already said and how you want readers to react to what you have written. Here are some different types of concluding paragraphs.

Look to the Future

> Nobody who played Pong back in the early 1970s would have believed how far video games would come in only a few decades. Video games now have improved graphics and are more popular than ever. With constantly improving technology, and with game designers' creativity, video games are sure to change dramatically in the decades ahead.

Encourage Your Reader to Take Action

> Soccer players' serious injuries should be enough to convince people that artificial turf needs to go. The way the turf affects ball bounce is another strong reason to go back to using real, natural turf. However, stadium owners do not want to change because plastic grass costs less. If your local soccer stadium uses artificial turf, e-mail the manager and request a change back to grass.

Ask Your Reader a Question

> The differences between my two vacation spots are clear. The city where my sister lives has shows, shopping, and fancy restaurants. In contrast, my aunt's home has a lake to fish on and horses to ride. Which vacation would you rather take?

Activity A **Use the chart to take notes for your concluding paragraph. Then write your paragraph on a separate sheet of paper.**

Restated ideas:
Final thought:

Activity B **Exchange papers with a partner. Review each other's graphic organizers and concluding paragraphs. Give specific suggestions to your partner, and listen to his or her comments and opinions. Use these questions as a guide.**

✔ Did I restate my main points accurately?

✔ Did I leave my reader with a final thought on the subject?

✔ In your opinion, is my conclusion interesting? If not, what changes would you make?

✔ What else would you like to know about this topic?

Writing Model

An excellent compare-contrast essay. . .

✔ includes an introductory paragraph that names the two subjects

✔ has a clear thesis statement that gives the main idea of the essay

✔ gives examples and details in well-organized body paragraphs

✔ organizes details using the block method or point-by-point method

✔ includes transitions, such as *similarly, differs from,* and *in contrast*

✔ concludes effectively by briefly restating the main points and leaving the reader with a final thought

✔ maintains reader interest throughout

Below is part of a compare-contrast essay. Ask your teacher how long your essay should be.

Video Games: Past and Present

Can you imagine playing a video game that has no music, no fancy animation, and hardly any graphics—only two straight lines (for paddles) and a tiny square (for a ball)? Allan Alcorn and Nolan Bushnell designed this game, called Pong, back in 1972. It was an immediate success. Video games have changed tremendously since the 1970s, but today's flashy games are still designed to wow fans and attract new players.

In the 1970s, video games lacked the technological advances that we are used to today. Like Pong, many of the games created during this time had very basic graphics. Characters looked like blocky stick figures, and movement on the screen was choppy and slow. Sound effects were also basic. Realistic music and sounds were not a part of video games of this time.

Game designers of the 1970s created games on the only computer systems available: bulky machines that took up entire rooms. Then video game developers made the move from these large machines (mostly used in universities, technology companies, and the military) to video games that

The thesis statement names the two subjects—video games of the 1970s and of today.

This essay uses the block method. The writer first describes all of the features of one subject.

continued

could be played in arcades. Some of the arcade games were nearly six feet tall and weighed from 300 to 500 pounds. When Magnavox introduced the first video game console to be played at home in 1972, these consoles were more portable but still boxy. Controllers were large joysticks with a few buttons.

However, video games of the 1970s were very popular. People had never seen this kind of technology before and were excited about this new form of entertainment. Some games, such as Dungeons and Dragons, had been played with pencil and paper. Video games did not replace these pencil-and-paper games, but they became a popular pastime in the United States and, in later years, around the world. Players also enjoyed the fact that the games became slightly more difficult as the players improved. For instance, in some games an onscreen enemy sped up as the player improved. In other games, obstacles came up more often or became harder to navigate. Still other games allowed the player to move faster as his or her skill level increased.

Unlike the video games made in the 1970s, today's games are much more sophisticated because the technology has improved. Today's games have three-dimensional graphics, stereo sound, and realistic-looking characters. They are also much faster than the original video games. These modern video games have multiple, interactive levels. Some consoles even let gamers talk to and interact with other players online. Many of today's games are portable, and some are even small enough to fit in a pocket.

Throughout the essay, the writer follows the outline he created (see page 59). This paragraph covers subject I, point C—the popularity of 1970s video games.

A transition signals to the reader that the writer is moving on to the second subject. The last three paragraphs of the essay are not shown.

Assignment

Write a compare-contrast essay on two topics that matter to you. You may use the same two topics that you have worked on throughout this chapter, or you may choose new topics.

Writing a Story

You probably already know that a story, also called a narrative, tells a series of events with a beginning, middle, and end. There are many different kinds of stories. A story can be true or fictional. It can be a comedy, tragedy, mystery, or adventure. It can be a few paragraphs long, or it can fill a book.

LESSON ① Develop Ideas

> ★ **Follow these steps to plan your story: focus on an idea, decide on your purpose and elements, and plan the steps of the plot.**

Tip

To come up with ideas for a story, try any of the techniques you learned in Chapter 1, Lesson 1:

- *freewriting*
- *clustering*
- *listing*
- *brainstorming*

Follow these steps for planning your story. . .

✔ **Focus on an idea.** You may base your story on something that happened to you—a major accomplishment, a mix-up, or something you witnessed. If you prefer, your story can be completely made up.

✔ **Decide on your purpose.** Think about who will read your story. Do you want your reader to laugh, cry, think, or shiver in fear?

✔ **Determine the story elements.** List the **characters** (people and animals) in your story, and describe them. Describe the **setting**— when and where the story takes place. You may want to establish a **theme,** or deeper message, for the story.

✔ **Focus on conflict.** What problem or danger is at the center of your story? Without a conflict, your writing is just a description, not a story.

✔ **Plan your plot.** Decide on the events in your story, and list them in order.

Keep working on your story even if you have trouble with it. Use the Story Map on the next page to plan what will happen in your story, when it will happen, and why it will happen.

Story Map

Creating a Story Map like this one will help you develop a well-organized story with a beginning, middle, and end.

Idea getting stuck on a rock when the tide came in

Purpose show how scared I was when I got stuck; show how relieved I was when I was back on land again

Characters me, my brother Tim, my parents, a stranger

Setting the beach, summer, hot day

Conflict need to escape deep water

Theme unexpected dangers

Plot Events

1. sitting on beach with family—Tim and I want to walk on the rocks
2. huge rock separated from the shore by an ankle-deep stream of water
3. walk out to rock, stand there awhile, enjoying the waves
4. look back—the tide has come in—water is now rough and much deeper
5. woman on shore sees us, helps us—parents worried

During the drafting stage, you may decide to add, delete, or rearrange information in your story.

Activity A Read the list of broad topics below. Pick one that interests you. Think of an idea that is related to that topic and that you might be able to turn into a story. Write your idea on a separate sheet of paper.

- places you have visited
- a dramatic change
- a scary or funny situation
- a modern version of a fairy tale

Activity B On a separate sheet of paper, create a Story Map for a story of your own. You may use the idea you developed in Activity A or another idea. Use the Story Map on this page as a model.

Draw the Reader In

> ⭐ **Capture and hold your reader's attention by writing clearly and imaginatively.**

 Tech Tip

Keep an index card, notebook, or personal digital assistant with you to note ideas for your story.

Tips for Drafting Your Story

✔ **Decide on a point of view.** You can use the first-person point of view ("I ran to the rocks") or the third-person point of view ("Dani ran to the rocks"). However, don't switch confusingly from one to the other.

✔ **Include dialogue.** Put characters' words in quotation marks. Start a new paragraph each time the speaker changes.

✔ **Add rich sensory details.** What can the characters see, hear, smell, feel, and taste?

✔ **Stay organized.** Tell your story in **chronological order,** also called time order. Include transitions such as *first, then,* and *after that* to help your reader understand the sequence of events.

Notice how this writer draws the reader into the story.

The first sentence of this story sets the scene for what will happen. Notice the first-person point of view.

> I never imagined that something so fun could become so dangerous. My family was enjoying a warm summer day at Holiday Beach. I was ten years old, and my younger brother Tim was seven. We had already made a sand castle, played in the waves, collected shells, and buried our legs in the sand. I was looking for something different to do—something adventurous.

In the paragraphs on the next page, the writer uses dialogue to move the story along. Notice the sensory details about the setting.

Transition word helps readers understand how fast events are taking place.

I noticed the chain of rocks reaching out to the ocean. At the end of the chain, I saw the waves breaking on the rocks, sending splashes of water skyward. Suddenly, I knew what we could do.

I begged my parents, "Can Tim and I take a walk on the rocks?"

My mother hesitated but sighed, "Be very careful and don't be gone longer than a half hour. Be sure to stay in sight."

"Oh, Mom. Quit worrying!" I said. "I can take care of myself and Tim."

"Are you sure it's safe?" Tim asked. "Those rocks look sharp."

Begin a new paragraph each time there is a new speaker.

Activity A Look back at the Story Map you created in Lesson 1 of this chapter. On a separate sheet of paper, list some specific details for each bulleted item below to use in your story.

- characters (main character, other characters, dialogue)
- setting (time, place, sensory details)
- plot events (in chronological order)

Activity B On a separate sheet of paper, draft the first few pages of your narrative. Try to include some of the specific details from Activity A.

Activity C When you have completed Activity B, exchange papers with a partner. Use this checklist as a guide.

✔ Is my story's point of view consistent?
✔ What three words would you use to describe the main character?
✔ Is the order of events clear?

Describe the Action

⭐ To maintain interest in the middle of the narrative, allow the plot to unfold step by step to its highest peak of action, the climax.

Tips for Writing the Middle of Your Story

✔ **Show, don't tell.** Instead of writing "I felt scared," give your reader details that show the character's mood: "My knees trembled as I searched for help."

✔ **Flesh out the characters.** In other words, describe them more fully. What do they think and feel? How do they act? Why do they do what they do?

✔ **Add modifiers to tell your reader** *how* **things happen.** The sentence "Tim asked tearfully what we were going to do" gives the reader a better understanding than "Tim asked what we were going to do."

Writing That Tells

Few details and no dialogue

> After I assured Tim, we reached the rock. I thought it was great. We stayed for about 15 minutes, and as we turned to go, Tim got scared and asked what we were going to do. I was scared too because the water was deep enough to be over our heads.

Writing That Shows

Dialogue and precise sensory details

> I assured Tim, "Everything's fine." We walked about ten feet through ankle-deep water until we reached the rock.
>
> "Isn't this great?" I shouted as the cool ocean water sprayed us. Staring out to sea, we stood happily on the rock for 15 minutes or more.

Writing That Shows (continued)

> Then I remembered we had better go back before Mom and Dad became worried. As we turned to leave, I saw the panicked look on Tim's face. The tide had come in! Off the rock, the water was now clearly over Tim's head. I knew that I could swim the short distance back, but Tim was not yet a strong swimmer, especially in rough water.
>
> "What are we going to do now?" he moaned, tears streaming down his cheeks.

The highlighted modifiers make this story more dramatic.

Do you see how showing gives a clearer, more immediate picture of the characters and their situation than telling? In the second version, the narrator uses specific details and dialogue to help the reader see the scene and get to know the characters.

Activity A **Write a brief passage that uses dialogue to capture each situation described below. Remember to show what the characters are like by what they say and do.**

1. You are angry with your younger sister. She has borrowed your favorite jacket without asking and has ruined it.

_____

_____

_____

_____

2. A friendly, outgoing person tries to make friends with a shy new student in school.

_____

_____

_____

3. Two members of a team have different attitudes about losing.

_____

_____

_____

_____

4. Two frightened campers hear a strange noise in the woods.

_____

_____

_____

_____

5. You walk into your cousin's house and realize that your family is throwing you a surprise party.

_____

_____

_____

_____

Activity B On a separate sheet of paper, draft the middle of your story. Use the plan you developed in Lesson 1, Activity B, and make sure the story picks up where you left off in Lesson 2, Activity B.

Activity C When you have completed Activity B, exchange papers with a partner. Read and evaluate each other's work, using the list of tips on the first page of this lesson as a guide.

Resolve the Conflict

> ★ **The ending of your story must resolve the conflict you introduced.**

Tech Tip

Consider turning your story into a script and then creating a short film that you can post to your smartphone. For instructions, enter the search terms "create podcast" or "create short film" into your favorite search engine.

A satisfying ending to a story. . .

✔ provides a solution for the main problem of the story
✔ follows a logical order
✔ shows that the main character has changed in some way

What if the story in this lesson ended with the two children stuck on the rock with the water rising? You would probably feel as if the writer let you down. When you write a story, make sure the reader knows the outcome. Read this conclusion to the story:

Is in chronological order

Solves the conflict

Shows how the main character changed

> Just then I heard a stranger yelling to us, "Are you kids okay? Do you need help?"
>
> "Yes," I shouted. "My brother needs some help."
>
> "Hold on, then," the kind voice replied. "I'll be right out."
>
> I swam to shore as a tall, red-haired woman helped Tim through the swirling water. It was a joy to hear my father's voice! He sounded relieved but angry.
>
> As Mom and Dad walked toward us, I realized how even a beautiful summer day can be dangerous. I decided that I would watch over Tim more carefully in the future.
>
> My parents ran to us and thanked the woman over and over. Dad turned to take our hands. As I saw the look on his face, I whispered to Tim, "This is going to be a long ride home!"

Activity A You are the editor of a website for new fiction. Each item below is the concluding paragraph to a short story. For each item, circle the letter of the best comment to make to the writer.

1.   Finally, I realized what the answer was. I would have to bargain with little Justin—or my babysitting days would be over. I read him three extra stories at bedtime; in exchange, he stopped screaming and went to bed quietly. Learning to compromise made me a better babysitter and a less stressed-out person.

  a. This conclusion does not include the solution to a problem.
  b. Events in this conclusion are not in chronological order.
  c. This conclusion does not explain how the main character has changed.
  d. Good job! This conclusion is fine as is.

2.   As Mark stood at the top of the mountain, he knew the climb had made him stronger and braver. He was nearly to the top! As he got ready to climb, he wondered if he would ever forget his first disastrous attempt.

  a. This conclusion does not include the solution to a problem.
  b. Events in this conclusion are not in a logical order.
  c. This conclusion does not explain how the main character has changed.
  d. Good job! This conclusion is fine as is.

3.   I waited for an hour until Romeo the cockatoo finally hopped back to the stoop to eat the breadcrumbs I had scattered. I caught him and, careful not to damage his feathers, returned Romeo to his cage. My sister never even knew the difference.

  a. This conclusion does not include the solution to a problem.
  b. Events in this conclusion are not in a logical order.
  c. This conclusion does not explain how the main character has changed.
  d. Good job! This conclusion is fine as is.

Activity B On a separate sheet of paper, draft the conclusion of your story. Make sure the story picks up where you left off in Lesson 3, Activity B. Then exchange papers with a partner. Read and evaluate each other's work, using the checklist on the first page of this lesson as a guide.

Writing Model

An excellent story. . .

✔ begins in a way that grabs the reader's attention

✔ "shows" the characters and setting to the reader by using rich details

✔ features realistic-sounding dialogue and a consistent point of view

✔ presents a central conflict that affects the main character and hints at a theme

✔ describes a plot in chronological order and includes transition words and phrases where they are needed

✔ has a satisfying conclusion that shows how the main character has changed and how the conflict was resolved

Below is a complete short story. Ask your teacher how many pages your short story should be.

Title and dialogue introduce the characters and get the plot moving.

Notice the third-person point of view.

The narrator shows the characters' excitement through description.

Earning a Badge

"I can't wait to go camping," Shane told Larry.

"Me, too," said Larry. "It's why I joined the scouting group in the first place."

To get their camping merit badges, Larry and Shane needed to go on a camping trip with their group. More than anything, Shane wanted to have the most badges, even though his scoutmaster had told him that he should learn a lesson with each badge he earned. "Sure," Shane thought, "but winning is more important."

The two boys arrived at Scoutmaster Mark's house as he was packing up his van for the trip. Coolers packed with ice and food, tents, first-aid kits, and other essentials were arranged in the back of the van. Smiles were on everyone's faces as they drove to the campsite, and they shouted songs at the top of their lungs.

"All right, scouts," the scoutmaster said as they arrived. "Let's get to work!"

continued

Quickly, the scouts unloaded the van and then marched toward a suitable campsite. They could smell the fresh air mixed with a sharp pine scent as they set up their tents near a stream. The troop separated to cook dinner and explore the area.

"Larry!" Shane yelled. "Scoutmaster Mark wants us to gather some water for the campsite."

"I'll be right there!" Larry said. He started running toward the sound of rushing water.

"Wait a second, Larry!" Shane shouted. He could feel his heart beating faster as he noticed that there was a dip in the ground that led to the river. "Larry could break his neck if he fell down in it," he thought.

Larry cried out as he tripped and fell. Then he moaned, his hands reaching up to rub the back of his head. They fell short, and he moaned louder. "It's my arm," he whimpered. "I think I broke it!"

Once Shane reached Larry, he mentally reviewed all the first-aid training they had received during scouting meetings. It didn't look as if Larry had any serious head, neck, or back injuries, and he was breathing. Shane untied his bandana and made a sling.

"Do you think you can get up and walk?" Shane asked him. Larry nodded. "Okay! One, two, three!" Shane said, cautiously pulling him up. They slowly walked back to the campsite.

Later, as Shane admired his camping badge, he decided that winning wasn't as important as knowing what to do in a crisis.

Assignment Write a short story. You can use the notes you took in this chapter, or you can invent a new story.

Writing a Persuasive Essay

Have you ever wanted to change the world—or just your corner of it? Writing persuasively can cause others to agree with you and even spur them to take action. In this chapter, you will write a persuasive essay.

LESSON ① Take a Stand

Tip

These words and phrases often signal that a statement is an opinion:

as I see it
better (or worse)
I believe
I think
it is clear that
must
most (or least)
probably
should

> ⭐ In a persuasive essay, you state a clear and strong **opinion,** which is a belief that cannot be proven true or untrue. You support that opinion with **facts,** or statements that are true and that can be checked.

Examples of Facts	Examples of Opinions
People keep birds and dogs as pets.	Birds make better pets than dogs.
Claude Monet, a French painter, lived from 1840 until 1926.	Monet was the most creative painter who ever lived.
Astronauts from 15 countries visited the International Space Station.	Space travel and exploration are worth the cost.

As you search for a persuasive topic. . .

✔ **Pick something that matters to you.** Your passion and enthusiasm will shine through in your writing.

✔ **Make certain your topic has two sides.** How can you be persuasive if everyone already agrees with you?

✔ **Consider your audience and purpose.** Who will read your essay, and what do you want your reader or readers to do?

✔ **Think about how you will gather evidence.** Will you do research in books or on the Internet? Will you interview experts or create a survey for people to fill out? Your evidence may include examples, anecdotes, quotations, and statistics.

Tech Tip

Newspapers publish persuasive essays called **editorials.** Enter the word editorial *into your favorite search engine to read editorials from around the world.*

✔ **Develop a thesis.** Write a one- or two-sentence statement that expresses your opinion and gives at least two reasons for it. For example, your thesis might be, "Our cafeteria needs to provide lunches that are more nutritious, more varied, and better tasting." You may need to change your thesis as you draft and revise.

✔ **Be sure your thesis is arguable.** Statements that express personal preference, such as "I like apples better than oranges," cannot be supported with logical reasons.

✔ **Make sure your thesis is controversial.** Reasonable people should disagree about your thesis. The statement "Slavery is unjust" is not controversial.

Activity

To help you decide on a persuasive essay topic, freewrite in response to one or more of the prompts below. Do your freewriting on a separate sheet of paper. Then write your thesis on the lines below.

If I Ran the World...

- If I ran the world, I would. . .
- It is unfair that. . .
- One stereotype that really bothers me is. . .
- I wish that. . .
- The best thing we, as students, can do is. . .
- I get angry about the issue of. . .
- I disagree that. . .
- One way to improve things is to. . .

Thesis for My Persuasive Essay: _____

_____

_____

_____

_____

Build Your Case

> ★ **To convince readers to accept your point of view, include supporting reasons and specific evidence.**

Tech Tip

Sometimes the shortest message is the most persuasive. How would you sum up your persuasive essay within a single text message?

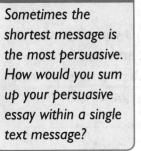

Use These Types of Evidence

✔ **Examples:** specific cases or instances

✔ **Facts:** statements that can be proved true

✔ **Quotations:** spoken or written words from an expert or authority

✔ **Statistics:** facts that contain numbers

✔ **Anecdotes:** brief stories that help you explain and expand on your thesis

Organize your reasons and evidence in an Argument Chart.

Thesis

A new park would make Clarkston a better place to live, both today and in the future.

Reason 1

Our community doesn't have enough recreation areas now.

Reason 2

Our community will need more recreation areas in the future.

Evidence

- Clarkston has only one small, wooded picnic area and one public ball field for 27,000 people.

- These areas are crammed with people every evening and weekend when the weather is fair.

Evidence

- Clarkston's growing population means that more people will use recreation areas.

- Because of cuts in physical education programs, students must exercise on their own.

Nobody likes to be bullied. Express your thoughts in persuasive yet polite language, as shown on the next page.

Maintain a Respectful Tone

Tone means "attitude." The strong example uses polite language and avoids insults.

> **Weak** It would be so dumb to open a shopping center on this land. You'd have to love asphalt and concrete to clutter our limited land with ugly buildings.
>
> **Strong** The citizens of the town would benefit much more from having a place to relax and exercise outdoors than they would from yet another shopping center.

Decide in which order you will present the details you are gathering. Some writers give the least important ideas first and work their way up to the most important ones. Others grab readers' attention with the most important idea and then list less important ones.

• Most important idea
• Second most important idea
• Third most important idea
• Least important idea

OR

• Least important idea
• Third most important idea
• Second most important idea
• Most important idea

Activity A Read each thesis and the two lettered statements below it. Circle the letter of the detail that offers stronger support. Then explain why on the line.

1. Without increased subway service to Center Arena, many ticketholders will never reach the concerts they plan to attend.

   a. Increased subway service is the only way to help concert ticket holders—there's just no other solution that's possible in this situation.

   b. Currently, ticket holders coming from some parts of the city have to wait over two hours to crowd onto a single subway train headed for the Center Arena area.

_____

2. Families who rent their homes should not be denied the privilege of owning a pet.

   a. A child who has a pet can learn the skills and responsibility of caring for a living thing.

   b. People are always saying that pets teach valuable lessons, and if enough people say something, it must be true.

   _____

3. Foreign language instruction should be available to students in elementary grades.

   a. Children like to dress in traditional costumes from different lands.

   b. Children who learn foreign languages also learn about and appreciate other cultures.

   _____

4. Older students should be encouraged to volunteer free time and study periods to help out in elementary school classrooms.

   a. This is one way to escape a boring, useless study period, so I guess it's worth a try.

   b. Students who help others learn develop confidence in their own knowledge of the subject.

   _____

5. The school lunch program should provide more menu choices.

   a. The food we get now is so disgusting that I wouldn't serve it to a pig.

   b. Many students want to select foods with less fat, such as more fruits and vegetables.

   _____

Activity B **On a separate sheet of paper, create a plan for your persuasive essay. Your plan can be an outline, a graphic organizer, or a list.**

Consider Counterarguments

> ★ Think about **counterarguments**—opinions and reasons that someone who disagrees with you might mention. **Respond** to these counterarguments by mentioning them in your essay and explaining why they are wrong. Then make a **final point** to convince your reader.

Here is a counterargument that might be made against the thesis presented in the beginning of Lesson 2.

> The cost of creating a park will make taxes far too high.

Response to Counterargument

> I realize that some people might be worried about tax increases. Actually, the tax commissioner states that taxes will be increased by less than $10 per household per year—a relatively small price to pay for a recreation area that will be free to all residents. Also, the more money we raise through fund-raising events and donations, the less money will have to come from taxpayers' pockets. Finally, the park would especially benefit Clarkston's children and, in that way, would be a sound investment in the future of our town.

Tip

This writer used the transition word actually *to signal that he is about to present a response to a counterargument.*

This writer makes a final point about the good consequences, or results, that a new park would have.

Ways to Make a Final Point

- Summarize the ideas in your essay.
- Ask a question that shows why your point of view is correct.
- Suggest an action that the reader can take.
- Describe good or bad consequences.

Activity A Read each opinion and possible objection. Then write a point you might make to counter the objection.

1. **Thesis:** Participating in school sports helps students become disciplined.
   Counterargument: Playing sports takes away from time that could be spent studying, doing volunteer work, or relaxing.

   Response: _____

   _____

2. **Thesis:** Math teachers should let students use calculators to solve problems and take tests. **Counterargument:** If students depend upon calculators, they will never develop their basic math skills.

   Response: _____

   _____

3. **Thesis:** School officials should let students wear any style of clothing they want. **Counterargument:** Having students wear similar clothing or uniforms prevents competition among peers.

   Response: _____

   _____

Activity B On a separate sheet of paper, draft a persuasive essay. Use the thesis you developed in Lesson 1 and the plan you developed in Lesson 2. Make sure your essay mentions at least one counterargument and provides a response to it.

Activity C When you have completed Activity B, exchange papers with a partner. Read and evaluate each other's work, using these questions as a guide:

✔ Could my thesis be stronger? If so, how should I change it?
✔ Do I give enough specific facts and relevant supporting details?
✔ Do I raise one or more counterarguments and answer them?

Writing Model

An excellent persuasive essay. . .

✔ introduces the topic in a clear and interesting way

✔ clearly presents an opinion in a thesis statement

✔ provides persuasive and relevant supporting reasons that are backed up by evidence, such as facts, quotations, statistics, examples, and anecdotes

✔ introduces at least one counterargument and responds to it

✔ maintains a respectful tone throughout

✔ makes a final point that is strong and memorable

Below is a complete persuasive essay. Ask your teacher how long your essay should be.

Clarkston Needs a Park: Show Your Support

The introduction presents a clear thesis statement that indicates the writer's opinion.

Like almost everyone, I enjoy going to the mall on a Saturday afternoon. However, I think we have paved over as much farmland around Clarkston as we should. I support the recent proposal to build a park on the west side of town. Malls are fun, but they offer few green spaces, provide few opportunities for sports and exercise, and add to air pollution. In contrast, a new park would make Clarkston a better and cleaner place to live, both today and in the future. The new park is an excellent idea for three reasons.

The writer supports Reason 1 with facts and examples about existing recreation areas.

First, our community doesn't have enough recreation areas now. With a population of over 27,000, Clarkston has only one small, wooded picnic area and one public ball field. These parks are crowded with people every evening and weekend when the weather is pleasant. As a result, our existing recreation areas look worn and shabby. With a new park, residents would have more options and space to enjoy a day outside. Also, the parks would be in better shape because they wouldn't be overused.

---

continued

Details about population and schools provide effective support for Reason 2.

Second, Clarkston will need more parks in the future. A growing population means that more people will use recreational areas. Also, because of cuts in physical education programs at our schools, students must exercise on their own. A new park would give students the opportunity to maintain physical activity.

The writer supports Reason 3 by explaining the connection between plants and cleaner air.

Finally, a new park would be good for the environment. Instead of paving over more open land, we could create a new park that provides more trees, bushes, and grass. Having more plants helps keep the air clean because plants take carbon dioxide out of the air and use it to make oxygen.

This paragraph presents a counterargument and responds to it effectively and respectfully.

Some opponents of the proposal say that creating a park will make local taxes too high. I can understand why people might worry about tax increases, but the risk in this case is small. Actually, the tax commissioner estimates that the new park will raise taxes by less than $10 per household per year—a small price to pay for a recreation area that will be free to all residents. Also, the more money we raise through fund-raising events and donations, the less money will have to come from taxpayers' pockets. Finally, the park would especially benefit Clarkston's children and, in that way, would be a sound investment in the future of our town.

The conclusion restates the thesis and the three reasons and then issues a call to action.

To meet the needs of the people of Clarkston today, to provide enough park space for our growing community tomorrow, and to help the environment, the proposal for a new park is a solid idea. I urge you to e-mail your local representative and express your support for a new park. The citizens of our town would benefit much more from having a place to relax and exercise outdoors than they would from having another shopping center.

Assignment

Now write your own persuasive essay. You may use the issue and the arguments that you brainstormed, or you may choose another issue.

Writing a Research Paper

A research paper is a detailed essay that showcases what you have learned on a particular subject. Choose a narrow topic that interests you, and follow a well-organized plan so the task of writing a research paper runs smoothly.

LESSON ① Choose a Topic and Locate Sources

> ★ To get started, **narrow your topic** until it fits the number of pages you have to write. Then **investigate research sources** to see how much information you can find.

Your teacher will tell you how many pages your research paper needs to be. He or she may assign you a topic or let you choose. This graphic organizer shows how one student narrowed a topic.

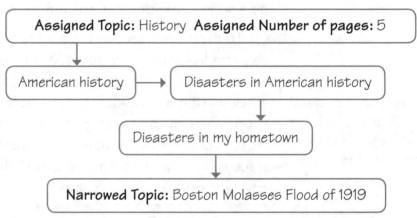

Assigned Topic: History **Assigned Number of pages:** 5

American history → Disasters in American history

Disasters in my hometown

Narrowed Topic: Boston Molasses Flood of 1919

The next step is to write a **thesis statement,** the main idea of your research paper. Your thesis may explain an idea or present an opinion. Avoid a thesis that merely states a fact.

Tip

You can revise your thesis as you research. You can even scrap your thesis and write a new one.

◻ Tech Tip

Verify facts in at least two sources. Websites that include these terms in the address are more likely to be trustworthy:

.gov (United States government)
.edu (schools and colleges)
.lib (libraries)

Stating a Fact The Boston Molasses Flood happened on January 15, 1919.

Expressing an Opinion Although the Boston Molasses Flood was a bizarre disaster, it reveals important information about daily life in the early 1900s.

Places to Do Research

✔ Visit a library or media center to look for books, encyclopedia articles, newspaper and magazine articles, and documentaries on your topic. Ask a reference librarian for help.

✔ Check the Internet for websites, articles, audio files, and video.

✔ Collect a variety of **primary sources.** Those are firsthand accounts, such as letters, speeches, and autobiographies.

✔ Look for **secondary sources.** These accounts are based on primary sources. Secondary sources include encyclopedia articles and biographies.

Create a source card for each source of information that you find.

Source Card (Book)

Number the source card in the upper right corner.

> 1
>
> Puleo, Stephen. <u>Dark Tide: The Great Boston Molasses Flood of 1919</u>. Boston: Beacon Press, 2003.

Source Card (Website)

> 2
>
> <u>What Caused the Great Boston Molasses Flood?</u> Updated 2008. Massachusetts Historical Society. Accessed May 2, 2008. <http://www.masshist.org/library/faqs.cfm#flood>

Your source cards will help you stay organized as you take notes. Find at least four sources on your topic, so you can learn different facts and details. Try to use multiple types of sources.

Activity A   For each general topic listed below, think of two specific topics that you might like to research. Write your answers on a separate sheet of paper.

1. transportation

2. the Internet

3. movies

4. sleep

5. nutrition

6. unusual places

7. sports

8. festivals

Activity B   On a separate sheet of paper, create a graphic organizer like this one. In the first box, write a general topic from Activity A, or think of your own. In the second box, list several narrower topics until you find one that interests you. Write your thesis statement in the third box.

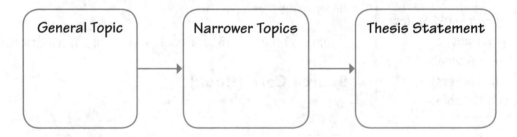

General Topic → Narrower Topics → Thesis Statement

Activity C   Reread the thesis statement you wrote in Activity B. Find sources that might help you write a research paper based on that thesis. You might find sources online, at a library or media center, or in your classroom. Then create at least two source cards. Use the examples on the second page of this lesson as models.

> ★ **Choose your sources carefully. Then read them, and record essential information on note cards.**

Before you take notes, decide which of the sources you have found are right for your research paper.

Questions to Ask About Research Sources

✔ **Is this source relevant to my thesis statement?** Don't waste your time with interesting but unrelated material.

✔ **Is this source up to date?** Check the copyright page (after the title page) or look for a "last updated" reference.

✔ **Is this source reliable?** Most books have been checked and corrected by editors. Some websites are the work of only one person. Check key facts in at least two sources.

For each source, create note cards that record **essential information** from that source. Include key facts, details, dates, or names to use in your paper. Write information about one subtopic or key idea per card. Include page numbers if they are available.

Tip

Topics related to technology, science, and sports often require up-to-date sources. Topics related to history or literature may not require sources that have been recently updated.

Source Card

Write the number of the source card in the right-hand corner.

> 3
>
> Knox, Robert. "The Untold Story of Boston's Great Molasses
>
>   Flood." <u>Boston Globe</u> 11 Jan. 2004: A1.

Note Card with Quotation

> 3
>
> "The molasses tank was 50 feet high and 90 feet in diameter.
>
> It held over 2 million gallons of molasses." (p. A1)

Ways to Record Information

✔ **Quote** the exact words of the source. Put the words within quotation marks.

✔ **Paraphrase** the source by restating it in your own words. A paraphrase is about the same length as the original passage.

Here is a note card that paraphrases the information on the previous page about the size of the molasses tank.

Note Card with Paraphrase

> 3
>
> The sweet, sticky syrup was contained in a gigantic vat.
>
> (p. A1)

Quoting and paraphrasing accurately helps you to avoid plagiarism.

Facts About Plagiarism

✔ **Plagiarism** means presenting someone else's ideas as your own. If you copy words from a source without explaining who wrote or said them, you are plagiarizing.

✔ Plagiarism is dishonest. It can cause you to receive a zero on an assignment or even to fail a class.

✔ To avoid plagiarizing, always quote, summarize, and paraphrase accurately. Tell your reader where you found the information.

✔ If you are taking notes from an online source, avoid cutting and pasting sentences or paragraphs into your paper. Instead, write or type the information in your own words.

Original Source

> After the molasses flood, lawmakers improved safety standards for buildings.
>
> —Rachel Pearson, "Effects of Boston's Molasses Flood," *Boston Journal,* May 2007, p. 14

Note Card with Plagiarized Information

> After the disaster, people improved safety standards for
> construction.

The information in this index card is plagiarized because the researcher has taken a phrase ("improved safety standards") without saying where those words came from. The source number and page number are also missing.

Organizing Your Paper

✔ Create source cards and note cards.

✔ Instead of trying to remember everything you have read all at once, put your note cards in an order that makes sense.

✔ Write your paper in the order of the note cards.

Activity A **Read the thesis and the paragraphs below. Then practice note-taking by writing quotations and paraphrases that you feel would help a student writing on that thesis. Write your notes on note cards or on a separate piece of paper.**

Thesis: Although the Boston Molasses Flood was a bizarre disaster, it reveals important information about daily life in the early 1900s.

1.   Fifty feet tall and ninety feet wide, the vat was built in 1915. The structure held over 2 million gallons of molasses. Why did anyone need so much molasses? The Purity Distilling Company planned to convert the molasses into industrial alcohol. The alcohol would be used to manufacture weapons—an important and profitable industry, especially during World War I. The vat sat on waterfront property in the North End, which at the time was the most crowded neighborhood in the extremely crowded city of Boston.

—Source 4 (David E. Samuelson, "Boston Historians Remember the Great Molasses Flood," *The Boston Record*, 14 January 2007, page B2)

2. In 1915, the Purity Distilling Company constructed a 50-foot-high steel tank in Boston's crowded North End neighborhood. The massive structure could hold two and a half million gallons of molasses. On Wednesday, January 19, 1919, the tank exploded. A flood of molasses rushed down Commercial Street through the North End. Soon, the sticky mess covered two city blocks.

—Source 5 (Historical Society of New England, <u>Was there really a molasses flood in Boston?</u>, <http://www.nehist.org/flood_of_1919>

3. Although molasses is a sticky, honey-like substance, that day the wave moved at approximately 35 miles per hour. Children on their way home from school got picked up and carried by the flood, including a young boy named Anthony. At first Anthony stayed on the surface of the molasses. Then he sank into the goo, which clogged his nose and throat. He lost consciousness. When he woke up, his sisters were staring at him, terrified.

—Source 6 (Anne Marie Montgomery, "The Molasses Disaster of 1919," <u>New England History Magazine</u>, August 2008, p. 32)

Activity B **On separate note cards, begin taking notes for your research paper.**

1. On each note card, list the number of the source card (so you don't have to write the title and author each time).
2. Quote or paraphrase essential information that relates to your thesis statement.
3. Include page numbers if your source has them.

Summarize and Synthesize Information

> ⭐ As you take notes for your research paper, you will **summarize** and **synthesize** information so you can explain ideas without unnecessary details.

When you **summarize** information, you give the main points of a text without any extra information. A summary is much shorter than the text it is based on.

Original Text

This text has lots of interesting details, but you don't need to know those details to understand the main idea.

> Commercial Street. It loops around . . . Copp's Hill from the Charlestown Bridge, east and south, to link with Atlantic Avenue. It roars with traffic—and it did so in 1919, but with different sounds. Instead of the thunder of today's diesels, there was the unmuffled blat of loaded lorries with solid rubber tires, the endless clop of work horses pulling freight wagons and, over all, the roar of the relatively new elevated railway—the "El"—that for years kept Commercial Street in shadow.
>
> —Edwards Park, "Without Warning, Molasses in January Surged Over Boston," <u>Smithsonian Magazine</u>

Tech Tip

Ask your teacher if it is permissible to add photographs, charts, graphs, or diagrams to your research paper. If you include a visual that someone else created, include a source line at the bottom, so readers will know where the information is from.

Summary

> The street where the molasses flood happened was busy back in those days, and it is still busy today.

When you **synthesize** information, you combine information you already know with new ideas. You break down a topic into its important parts and then put it together in a new way.

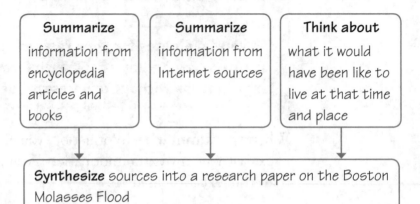

Summarize	Summarize	Think about
information from encyclopedia articles and books	information from Internet sources	what it would have been like to live at that time and place

Synthesize sources into a research paper on the Boston Molasses Flood

As you summarize and synthesize, keep your language formal. Informal language and slang terms do not belong in a research paper. They make your writing seem sloppy and rushed.

Activity A **Read each paragraph, circling or highlighting key words and phrases. Then circle the letter of the best summary.**

1. Some of the first people to help were sailors from the USS *Nantucket*, which was docked close by. More than 100 sailors ran to the scene of the molasses flood. Some waded up to their knees in the sticky, sweet-smelling goo. Police officers, Red Cross nurses, and soldiers also arrived. They performed many tasks—treating the injured, keeping them warm, and keeping passersby out of the way.

a. The molasses was knee-deep in some areas.
b. The sailors were the most helpful of all.
c. Hundreds of people rescued and cared for the injured.

2. It took months to clean up the neighborhood. Because the streets were made of bumpy cobblestones, the gunk got stuck in the gaps. Molasses got into people's homes and cars as well as into neighborhood schools, churches, theaters, and businesses. The water in the harbor smelled of molasses until the summer.

a. Cleaning up the molasses took a great deal of time.
b. Schools and churches were affected.
c. The sticky residue made streets hard to navigate.

Activity A *continued*

3. Local newspapers, magazines, and websites run special stories and photographs on the anniversary of the molasses flood. Authors have written books about the disaster. Nearby historical societies give special presentations on the flood and how it changed the city.

a. The flood changed the city.

b. Books about the Boston Molasses Flood are available.

c. People today still remember the Boston Molasses Flood.

Activity B

On a separate sheet of paper, create a graphic organizer like the one below. Use the organizer to summarize the information you have collected on your research topic. Add boxes for more sources if you need to. As you create your summaries, ask yourself these questions:

- Which information in this source would be most helpful to someone unfamiliar with this topic?

- What did I learn from this source?

- Which facts or details in this source helped me to understand my topic better?

- Which facts or details from this source will I include in my research paper? Why?

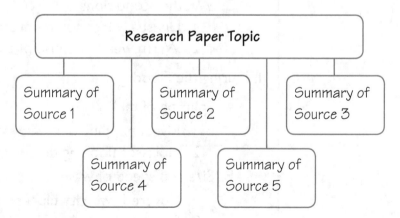

Activity C

On a separate sheet of paper, list at least three formats you could use to synthesize the information you have learned on your topic into something new. For ideas, reread the tip on page 94.

LESSON 4 Make an Outline

> ★ Planning makes writing easier. A formal or informal **outline** is a kind of road map to use as you write your research paper.

You learned in Chapter 6, Lesson 2 that an **outline** is an organized list of information. Your teacher may require you to include a formal outline with the final draft of your research paper. Even if you aren't required to create an outline, doing so can help you get organized.

Formal Outline

Each point should be either a phrase (as shown here) or a complete, punctuated sentence. Do not mix the two styles.

The Boston Molasses Flood of 1919

I. Before the Flood

    A. North End neighborhood
        1. Most crowded in the city
        2. Most people poor immigrants
    B. Purity Distilling Company's molasses tank
        1. Molasses used for industrial purposes
        2. Over 2 million gallons in tank
    C. Weather conditions
        1. Unusually high temperatures for January
        2. Warm weather cause of expansion of molasses

II. During the Flood

    A. Splitting of tank
        1. Rivets popping out
        2. Molasses flooding downtown Boston
    B. Size and speed of wave
        1. Covered two city blocks
        2. Estimated speed of 35 miles per hour
    C. People and animals in danger
        1. Children on way home from school
        2. Horses pulling wagons

Informal Outline

> **Title:** The Boston Molasses Flood of 1919
>
> Introduction and thesis

> **Part 1:** Before the Flood—Set the scene by describing where the tank was, what it was used for, and what the day was like.

> **Part 2:** During the Flood—Explain how dangerous the flood was, and tell about the people and animals it threatened.

> **Part 3:** After the Flood—Describe the rescue and cleanup efforts. Then explain changes in safety regulations.

> **Conclusion**—Tell the lasting impact that the flood had.

The last part of your research paper is the Works Cited page. Simply arrange your source cards in alphabetical order by author. Then copy the information from the cards onto one sheet of paper. Double-space each line, and indent all lines except for the first line of each entry.

Activity **Gather your note cards, and put them in a logical order. Then create a formal outline of the information that will be in your research paper. Use this checklist to evaluate your work.**

✔ Does my outline have the same structure as the example on the previous page?

✔ Do I need to add any points? (If there is a point A, there must be a point B; if there is a point 1, there must be a point 2.)

✔ Does every point in the outline connect to my thesis statement?

✔ Are the parts of the outline in a logical order?

WORKSHOP) Writing Model

An excellent research paper. . .

✔ focuses on a narrow topic

✔ presents a thesis statement and supports it with information from a variety of reliable primary and secondary sources

✔ accurately quotes, paraphrases, and summarizes information

✔ avoids plagiarism and properly credits all sources

✔ includes a list of Works Cited

Below is part of a research paper. Ask your teacher how long your paper should be.

A Unique Disaster

Natural and man-made disasters are familiar to all of us—at least from television and newspaper reports. Once in a while, however, a disaster occurs that is unique as well as tragic. Such an event happened on January 15, 1919, when a huge tank containing two and a half million gallons of molasses broke and flooded Boston's North End neighborhood, killing 21 people and injuring hundreds. Although the Boston Molasses Flood was a bizarre disaster, it reveals important information about daily life in a big American city in the early 1900s.

The thesis is neither too broad nor too narrow. It focuses on one particularly unusual disaster.

Today, the site of the disaster is a park. On January 15, 1919, however, the North End was a slum where tens of thousands of Italian immigrants lived in dark, narrow apartment buildings called tenements. Because of a huge wave of new immigrants, "crowding in the North End had become horrific" (Puleo 33). Many of these newcomers were not yet citizens and were still learning English, so they did not participate in Boston politics. Therefore, when a 50-foot-high storage tank to hold molasses was built in the North End in 1915, no local residents protested the potentially dangerous structure (Knox A1; Mason 109).

The writer uses an in-text citation to credit the source of the quotation.

continued

The Boston Molasses Flood had significant effects on daily life in Boston and in other large American cities. Hugh Ogden, the official who conducted the hearings investigating the disaster, wrote a report that was sharply critical of those who built and inspected the tank. He wrote, "A proper regard for the appalling possibility of damage to persons and property contained in the tank in the case of accident demanded a higher standard of care" (Puleo 227). Because of the disaster and the report, governments strengthened safety standards for construction ("What Caused"). Several states passed laws that required engineers to pass a certification test to prove that they were qualified (Mason 110). Finally, the disaster showed newcomers to the United States that they needed to become active in politics so they and their neighborhoods would be safe (Puleo 57).

The writer credits the sources of quoted, paraphrased, and summarized information. The source about government standards does not include the author's name, so the writer cited a shorter version of the title.

Works Cited

Knox, Robert. "The Untold Story of Boston's Great Molasses Flood." Boston Globe 11 Jan. 2004: A1.

Mason, John. "The Molasses Disaster of 1919." Yankee Magazine Jan. 1965: 52–53, 109–111.

Park, Edwards. "Without Warning, Molasses in January Surged Over Boston." Smithsonian Magazine Nov. 1983: 212–218.

Puleo, Stephen. Dark Tide: The Great Boston Molasses Flood of 1919. Boston: Beacon Press, 2003.

This partial Works Cited list shows how to credit a newspaper article, a magazine article, and a book. See page 87 to learn how to credit a website.

Assignment **Use the notes you took throughout this chapter to write a research paper. Include a Works Cited list as the last page of your paper.**

Chapter 10

WORKSHOP

Strategies for School Success

Writing is part of your everyday life as a student—in English class and in other classes. Learning some writing strategies can help you do better work in less time, earn higher grades, and feel more confident in your abilities.

LESSON ① Write a Summary

 A **summary** is a shortened version of a longer work that covers only the main idea and key points.

You may need to write a summary of. . .

✔ a book you have read, so you can write a book report

✔ a story or essay you read in English class

✔ a textbook chapter for social studies class

✔ a science experiment, so you can write a lab report

✔ a documentary, movie, or video clip that you watched

In a **plot summary,** you describe only the most important characters and events in a story, novel, play, movie, or documentary. Here is an example.

Characters	The documentary *Spellbound* follows eight middle-school students who want to compete in the National Spelling Bee.
Location	The film takes place in the different parts of the country where the students live, and then it moves to Washington, D.C., for the finals. The viewer meets all eight students and their families.
Main problem	All the students want the fame, the satisfaction, and the money that comes with being national champion, but only one of them can win.

Tips for Writing a Plot Summary

- State where the story takes place and who the most important characters are.

- Describe the conflict, or main problem, and how it is resolved.

- Provide only as much detail as is needed to understand the plot.

- Use your own words to combine ideas in clear sentences.

Tips for Writing a Nonfiction Summary

- Include key terms, names, and dates.

- Try to express the main idea in one sentence.

- Eliminate details that are not related to the main idea.

Activity A **Write a plot summary of a short story or book that you have read. Use the form below to plan your summary. Then use other sheets of paper to draft, revise, and write a final version.**

Title: _____

Kind of story (adventure, mystery, etc.): _____

Setting (where and when the action takes place): _____

_____

Conflict (main problem): _____

_____

Main events: _____

_____

_____

How the conflict is resolved: _____

_____

Summary: _____

_____

Activity B **Read these passages from science and social studies textbooks. On the lines below, write a summary of each paragraph.**

1.   All substances are made of molecules that are constantly in motion. Molecules move around randomly, without a pattern. The random motion causes the same average number of molecules to be present in different places. When two substances combine, diffusion may happen. To understand diffusion, imagine a glass of clear water. If you add a drop of food coloring to the water, the coloring molecules are bunched up in one area. Over time, the coloring molecules start spreading out through the water.

_____

_____

_____

_____

2.   Gradually, from the time of the first settlements to that of the growing colonies, British settlers in America were separating from their homeland. By the mid-1700s, colonists felt quite independent of Great Britain. Instead of relying heavily on British products, the colonists were able to make many of their own goods. Because workers were able to grow more and make more than their families needed, they wanted to sell what was left over. As British subjects, however, the colonists had to obey British laws designed to keep the colonists tied to the British market. Restraint of trade was just one of the frustrations that led to the Revolutionary War.

_____

_____

_____

_____

Write for an Essay Test

> When taking an essay test, notice and underline **key words** in the essay question that tell you what to do. Then plan, draft, and revise your response.

Tip

Think about how much time you will devote to each essay question. Divide the amount of time you have by the number of essay questions to figure out how much time you should spend on each question.

First, read quickly through the test directions. Try to understand what you are expected to do on the test as a whole before you begin writing answers. Then read the first essay question again and underline key words that describe what you are required to do.

Examples of Key Words

- **Analyze** Look at all the parts that make up a whole. Think about how the parts work together to make up the whole.

- **Compare/Contrast** Talk about the similarities and differences between two (or more than two) people, places, things, ideas, or situations.

- **Describe** Give a detailed account. Talk about characteristics, features, or anything else that distinguishes something or someone. Add facts and details that help the reader visualize what you describe.

- **Define** Tell what the term or expression means. Give details and examples if possible.

- **Explain** Help the reader understand what you know about the topic. Use examples and facts. Make sure the parts of the explanation are in a logical order.

- **Interpret** Give your opinion about the meaning or the importance of something. Think about all the details you know and draw a conclusion.

Steps to Answering an Essay Question

✔ **Make notes** about items that you will include in your response. Write in the margins or on the back of the test sheet. The notes will help you decide how to organize and focus your answer.

✔ **Draft your response.** Use terms in your answer that were included in the question. If the essay question asks you to name three *parts* of something, you might write, "The most important *part* is. . ." and later "The second most important *part* is. . ."

✔ **Revise.** Delete any unnecessary information. Make sure your response answers all parts of the question.

✔ **Proofread** your essay for correct spelling, capitalization, punctuation, grammar, and usage.

Activity A **Read each question below, and underline key words. On the lines, make notes to help you plan your response. On a separate sheet of paper, write an answer of at least one paragraph for each question.**

1. Define the term *democracy*. Give three characteristics of a democratic society.

_____

_____

_____

_____

2. Describe a favorite character from a story, television program, or movie. Explain why you like this character.

_____

_____

_____

_____

_____

3. In one or two paragraphs, analyze the following poem. Be sure to discuss the words the poet chose and the way the poem makes a reader feel.

> **The Eagle**
>
> He clasps the crag with crooked hands:
>
> Close to the sun in lonely lands,
>
> Ringed with the azure world, he stands.
>
> The wrinkled sea beneath him crawls;
>
> He watches from his mountain walls,
>
> And like a thunderbolt he falls.
>
> —Alfred, Lord Tennyson

_____

_____

_____

_____

Activity B **Review the answers you wrote for Activity A. Choose the one that you believe is strongest, and exchange it with a partner. Evaluate each other's work using the checklist below.**

✔ Have I provided accurate information?

✔ Is the information complete, or do I need to add more?

✔ Have I included enough details?

✔ Is all information in my answer related to the test question?

Write for Other Subjects

⭐ **When you complete writing assignments in your other classes, use your skills as a writer to showcase the subject knowledge you have gained.**

You may need to write. . .

✔ an explanation of division of decimals for math class

✔ a research paper for social studies class

✔ a lab report for science class

✔ an essay or a presentation for another class, such as music, speech, health, art, or computer science

Think about what you have learned about your topic from your reading, research, and classroom discussions and activities. Use the writing skills you have developed in this class to present what you know in a clear, concise, interesting way.

Tech Tip

*If you decide to do research on the topic, take a look at a **visual dictionary** online. These sites include helpful photographs, diagrams, and cross-sections. They also include labels with specific terms and names.*

Tips for Writing About Social Studies

- Show that you understand the time period you are writing about—how people lived, what was happening, and so on.

- As you describe events, maintain correct chronological order.

- Demonstrate that you know where events took place and why they were important.

- Show your knowledge of social studies by including related and specific details.

Example of a Social Studies Assignment

> **Question** Imagine that you are 12 years old and live in the American colonial period. Describe your feelings about one aspect of your life, such as family, friends, school, chores, or entertainment.

How would you answer this question? On the next page, you will see three different responses.

Incorrect Example

Refers to things that had not been invented in colonial times

> My name is Greta, and I live in Pennsylvania. I do not enjoy school because we have too few movies. We study too much about the world wars.

Weak Example

Too general and few details

> I am Greta, and I live in the Pennsylvania colony. I really love school because I get to learn a lot. I would not learn so much if I had to stay home and take care of our farm. The classroom isn't fancy, but my teacher is very dedicated and willing to use the materials she has to teach us.

Strong Example

Exact details about where schools were located and what subjects were taught

> My name is Greta, and I live in the Pennsylvania colony. Though I have to ride my horse, Thunder, several miles each day to get to school, the trip is worth it. I am grateful to be reading, studying Latin, learning arithmetic, and practicing my writing. I am getting very good at reciting, and my bookkeeping is improving.

The strong example is longer than the first two, but length alone does not make a better answer. What is important is to provide details that are exact, correct, and related.

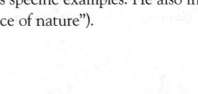

Tips for Writing About Science

- If you are explaining a concept, such as ecosystems or magnetism, use details and information to explain it fully.

- If possible, use examples that are easy for your audience to understand.

- Introduce science terms and definitions when needed.

As you read the example on the next page, notice how the student includes specific examples. He also introduces and defines a concept ("balance of nature").

Example of a Science Assignment

Question What is an ecosystem? Explain how an ecosystem functions.

Strong Example

The writer uses detailed examples to answer the question fully.

An ecosystem consists of a community of plants and animals living together and the nonliving environment with which they interact. Ecosystems can be large or small—the ocean, a forest, a pond, or a terrarium. The living members of an ecosystem depend upon one another as well as upon the environment for survival. For an individual species to survive in an ecosystem, the relationships the species has with the living and nonliving aspects of the environment must remain stable. This stable condition is sometimes called the "balance of nature." For example, there can be no more rabbits than there are plants for food to maintain them. Plants must have enough sunlight, soil, and water. If the rabbits eat too many of the plants, then both the plants and the rabbits will die out.

Activity A On a separate sheet of paper, write a paragraph to answer each question. If necessary, use books, encyclopedia articles, or online resources to find important facts and details.

1. Describe at least three ways that butterflies and moths differ.

2. Summarize one of the important events that led to the American Revolution. Explain why it was important.

3. Explain how penicillin was discovered and why the discovery was important.

Activity B Review the paragraphs you wrote for Activity A. Choose the one that you believe is strongest, and exchange it with a partner. Evaluate each other's work.

Writing Model

An excellent response to an essay question. . .

✔ gives a complete answer to the question

✔ shows the writer's knowledge about the subject

✔ uses key words from the question

✔ has a clear structure that makes sense to the reader

✔ defines terms as needed and only includes necessary information

Below is a response to the question, "Define the term *photosynthesis*, and explain how plants use it. Then tell why photosynthesis is important."

The writer broke his response to this two-sentence question into two paragraphs.

> Photosynthesis is the process that almost all plants use to make food. This process involves changing one kind of energy into another. For example, plants get water from the rain or from other sources, such as nearby rivers, lakes, or streams. In addition, plants get carbon dioxide from the air. Finally, they get energy from the heat and light of the sun. Plants combine these elements in order to grow.

The writer repeats some of the key terms from the question.

> Photosynthesis is important because all life on our planet depends on it. Without photosynthesis, plants would die. Without plants, all plant-eating animals would die. Without plants and animals, humans would not have any food to eat. Therefore, humans could not exist without the food that photosynthesis provides.

Assignment Search your literature, social studies, or science textbook for essay questions. Find one that interests you, and write a response to it. Then trade papers with a partner, and check each other's work. Even if you are unfamiliar with the subject matter, you can review your partner's work to see if it has a clear structure. Also, check for errors in spelling, grammar, and punctuation.

Writer's Handbook

CAPITALIZATION

- Capitalize the first word of a sentence and the pronoun *I*.

  My father and I enjoy cooking.

- Capitalize proper nouns—the names of people—including their titles, if the title appears before the name.

  Aunt Emma

  Mr. Sprague

  Dr. Ana Menendez

- Do not capitalize the title if it is used as a common noun.

  My aunt is a judge.

- Capitalize the days of the week, months of the year, holidays, historical events, and special events. These words are also proper nouns.

  Independence Day is on July 4. If this day falls on the weekend, most workers get a day off on the previous Friday or the following Monday.

- Do not capitalize names of seasons.

  This fall seemed more like spring.

- Capitalize geographical names: cities, states, regions, countries, continents, planets, bodies of water, and landmarks.

  We took a ski vacation to the West, in the Rocky Mountains.

- Do not capitalize the name if it is a common noun or a direction word.

  To the east of Lake Champlain is the state of Vermont.

- Capitalize the names of buildings, structures, streets, businesses, and organizations.

  From the top of the John Hancock Tower, I could see Atlantic Avenue and Faneuil Hall Marketplace.

- Capitalize the first, last, and important words in a title of a work, such as a book, poem, song, movie, article, or sculpture. (Do not capitalize *a, an, and, or, of, to, for,* or *by*.)

  "How to Have a Memorable Vacation"

A Proofread Sample

> this Spring, my family will take a trip
>
> to southern california. we plan to
>
> visit the san diego zoo, balboa park,
>
> and even tijuana, mexico.

ABBREVIATIONS

An abbreviation is the short form of a word or phrase. Abbreviations are frequently used to describe people's titles, times and dates, places, and measurements.

- Abbreviations of titles are acceptable in any type of writing.

    Mr. (Mister)   **Mrs. (Mistress)**

    Dr. (Doctor)

- Abbreviations for time are also acceptable in both formal and informal writing.

    A.M. (*ante meridiem*)

    P.M. (*post meridiem*)

- Do not use abbreviations of place names or measurements in formal writing.

    IL (Illinois)   **St. (Street)**

    km (kilometer)   **mi (mile)**

- Two types of abbreviations are acronyms and initialisms. An acronym is a word formed from letters in a phrase. Initialisms are similar to acronyms but cannot be pronounced as words. Both types of abbreviations often appear on the Internet.

    ASAP (as soon as possible)

    CIA (Central Intelligence Agency)

    DOJ (Department of Justice)

    IM (instant message)

    LOL (laugh out loud)

    NASA (National Aeronautics and Space Administration)

    scuba (self-contained underwater breathing apparatus)

    WHO (World Health Organization)

A Proofread Sample

> Dr.   New York
> ~~Doctor~~ Perkins arrived in ~~NY~~ at
>   miles
> 9:30 A.M. He lives 3,500 ~~mi~~ away in
> United Kingdom
> the ~~UK~~.

NUMBERS

- Numbers from zero to nine are usually written as words. Numbers 10 and over are usually written as numerals.

    eight   **74**

- Some very large numbers are usually written with a combination of words and numerals. Numbers that can be written as two words may also be written as words instead of numerals.

  4.5 billion

  eight thousand or 8,000

- Always use words, not numerals, to begin a sentence.

  Three sisters won the prize.

- Use numerals to indicate decimals, percentages, chapters and pages, time, telephone numbers, dates, addresses, statistics, and amounts of money.

  $7.99   **12.5 percent**

  page 233   **555-0812**

- If a sentence contains two or more numbers, write all of them as numerals or as words.

  Students ages 7 to 15 are invited to attend.

  Students ages seven to fifteen are invited to attend.

  A Proofread Sample

  > The group needed to raise ~~fifteen~~ ¹⁵ percent more than last year to reach its goal of ~~seven thousand~~ $7,800 ~~eight hundred dollars.~~

End Marks

- Use a period to end most sentences (statements, mild commands or requests, and indirect questions).

  Mrs. Baxter distributed the report cards.

  I wonder where he is.

- Use a question mark to end a direct question.

  When did you arrive?

  Do you know how to get there?

- Use an exclamation point only after a strong command, a sentence that expresses excitement, or an exclamation.

  Don't press that button!

  No way! She couldn't have done it by herself!

  A Proofread Sample

  > Did I tell you about my strange dream? I wonder what made me have such a nightmare! What a scary situation it was!

Apostrophes

- Add an apostrophe and *-s* to show possession by a singular noun.

  Thomas's sneakers are the same as Andrew's.

- Add just an apostrophe to show possession by a plural noun.

  The carpenters' tools are in the Donahues' garage.

- Add an apostrophe and *-s* to show possession by a plural noun that does not end with *s*.

  The manager listened to the women's and men's concerns.

- Use an apostrophe to stand for missing letters in contractions.

  We'll go if they don't get here soon. (we will; do not)

- Do not use an apostrophe in the words *hers*, *his*, *ours*, *yours*, or *theirs*. Use *its* when you mean "belonging to it"; use *it's* when you mean "it is."

  The problem is hers, but its solution depends upon all of us.

- Do not use an apostrophe to show a plural.

  The monkeys screeched, and the parrots shrieked.

A Proofread Sample

The pack of dogs' stalked the quiet neighborhood. First, they chased the Pirella's cat. Then they trampled Mrs. Martins garden.

Commas

- Use commas to separate three or more items in a series.

  You will need scissors, glue, and construction paper.

- Use a comma to separate two or more adjectives before a noun.

  I breathed the hot, humid air.

- Use a comma to separate the independent clauses of a compound sentence.

  The lights dimmed, and the crowd fell silent.

- Use a comma after an introductory phrase.

  Marching proudly, the band members led the parade.

- Use commas to separate an appositive from the rest of the sentence.

  Benjamin Franklin, an inventor, was well known.

- Use commas to separate from the rest of the sentence any words that offer additional information.

  Benjamin Franklin, who had many different talents, was a publisher and printer.

- Use commas to set off the name of someone being addressed.

  We are so glad that you could make it to the party, Aunt Louise.

- Use commas to set off *yes*, *no*, and other interrupters and transition words.

  No, I did not watch that show last night.

  My brother, however, told me that the show was funny.

- Use commas to separate elements of addresses and dates.

  The meeting was held in Santa Fe, New Mexico, on the afternoon of April 17, 2008.

A Proofread Sample

The colonists demonstrated their anger on December 16, 1773. The British, who had imposed several restraints on the colonists, had recently placed a tax on tea. To protest the tax, angry colonists dumped tea into Boston Harbor.

Do not use commas. . .	Examples
between coordinate adjectives (If the adjectives make sense separated by *and*, insert the comma. If they sound odd, leave out the comma.)	**He wore a red flannel shirt with a pair of old blue jeans.**
when *and*, *but*, or *or* introduces a group of words that is not a complete sentence	**The band could have been delayed or could have been trying to solve a technical problem.**
if an appositive is necessary to the meaning of the sentence	**The publisher Benjamin Franklin was well known for his many inventions.**
if a phrase or clause contains necessary information	**Works that Benjamin Franklin published expressed his political and social views.**
if only the month and year of a date are named	**The meeting was held in September 2008.**

Semicolons

- Use a semicolon to separate two complete sentences that are closely connected in meaning (and not joined by *and*, *but*, or *or*).

   The package did not arrive until Friday; however, I had put it in the mail on Monday.

Colons

- Use a colon to introduce a list.

   Before you begin, wash these vegetables: lettuce, cucumber, pepper, celery, and tomato.

- Do not use a colon after an introduction unless that introduction is a complete sentence.

   Before you begin, wash the lettuce, cucumber, pepper, celery, and tomato.

Ellipses

- An ellipsis (three periods) shows a pause in dialogue or omitted words in quoted materials.

   "I didn't bring my homework because. . .my dog ate it," he said.

   According to the newspaper article, "Pluto was demoted to a dwarf planet. . ."

A Proofread Sample

> The aquarium opened at 9 A.M.ˏwe entered at 9:30. We saw the top attractions⸲sea lions, dolphins, and sharks.

Quotation Marks

- When you are copying someone's exact words, put those words inside quotation marks.

   The Revolutionary War hero Patrick Henry said, "Give me liberty or give me death."

- If the words you are quoting are not a complete sentence, you do not need to capitalize the first word of the quotation.

   My grandmother told me that when she was young, technology was "completely different from how it is now."

- Use quotation marks to show dialogue (the exact words of characters or people).

   "Let's get going! We're going to be late!" I told my mother and brothers.

- When writing dialogue, use an indent to begin a new paragraph each time the speaker changes.

>   **"Did you see that?" Jackie asked.**

>   **"No. What happened?" Travis answered.**

- If the speaker is named first, put a comma before the opening quotation marks. Capitalize the first word of the quotation if it is a complete sentence. Put a period or other end mark inside the closing quotation marks.

>   **Angelo mumbled, "There's something that I haven't told you."**

- If the quotation is the first part of the sentence, put the end mark inside of the closing quotation marks. Use a comma where you would normally use a period.

>   **"There's something that I haven't told you," Angelo mumbled.**

>   **"What is it?" Joanne asked.**

>   **"I'm scared of heights!" he howled.**

- If the speech is interrupted, enclose each part within quotation marks. Do not capitalize the second part of the quotation.

>   **"I cleaned out my locker yesterday afternoon," said Frederica, "which is something I have been meaning to do all month."**

>   **"Well," said Ed, "it still looks messy to me."**

A Proofread Sample

"where are we going Shauna asked.

"I think"said her brother"that this bus doesn't stop where we thought it did."

Punctuating Titles

- Use quotation marks to enclose titles of short works, such as short stories, articles, chapters, poems, and songs.

I read my little brother a story called "The Three Billy-Goats Gruff."

Our teacher showed us a magazine article called "Organization is the Key to Success" and another called "Homework Tips for Middle School Students."

Chapter 7 of our science textbook is called "Ecosystems."

In English class, we read a poem called "Sarah Cynthia Sylvia Stout Would Not Take the Garbage Out."

Janelle's favorite song is "She'll Be Comin' Round the Mountain When She Comes."

- Use underlining or italic type for titles of longer works, such as books, magazines, newspapers, movies, and plays.

Rich's favorite book is *Hatchet,* a novel by Gary Paulsen.

I bought my cousin a subscription to *Skateboarding Monthly.*

When my dad was a boy, he had a paper route, delivering copies of the *Arizona Republic.*

***Mary Poppins* was my favorite movie when I was little.**

Our class saw a play called *A Thousand Cranes.*

A Proofread Sample

My brother acted in the play "Peter Pan." He got a positive review in our local newspaper, the Braintree Forum. The best song in the play is "Never Smile at a Crocodile." A book called "Acting for Young Adults" helped him prepare for the performance.

SPELLING

Adding Endings

- For most words, just add the ending without making spelling changes.

fear + -less = fearless

- If a one-syllable word ends with a consonant preceded by a single vowel, and the ending begins with a vowel, double the final consonant. If the word has more than one syllable, double the final consonant only if the last syllable is stressed.

bat + -er = batter

orbit + -ed = orbited

admit + -ing = admitting

- If the word ends with a final silent *e* and the ending begins with a vowel, drop the final *e*. Keep the final *e* if the ending begins with a consonant.

shine + -y = shiny

spite + -ful = spiteful

- If the word ends with a consonant and -*y*, and the ending begins with any letter except *i*, change the *y* to *i*. If the word ends with a vowel and -*y*, just add the ending.

carry + -er = carrier

lonely + -ness = loneliness

employ + -ment = employment

A Proofread Sample

I am hopeing someday to be a singger. I think I have the major requirement—a pleaseing voice. My happyest childhood memories involvd music and songs, and I always carryed a tune.

Making Plurals

- To make most nouns plural, add -s.

doors	**houses**
apartments	**schools**

- If the noun ends with -s, -ss, -sh, -ch, -z, -zz, or -x, add -es.

bosses	**dishes**
lunches	**boxes**
wrenches	**atlases**
buses	**walruses**
bushes	**sixes**

- If the noun ends with a consonant and -y, change the y to i and add -es.

artery/arteries	**pony/ponies**
diary/diaries	**story/stories**

- For some nouns, change a final -f or -fe to -ves.

leaf/leaves	**loaf/loaves**
life/lives	**half/halves**
wife/wives	**wolf/wolves**
knife/knives	**scarf/scarves**

- Some nouns change spellings in singular and plural forms.

tooth/teeth	**foot/feet**
mouse/mice	**man/men**
child/children	**woman/women**
goose/geese	

- Some nouns keep the same spelling in singular and plural forms.

moose	**deer**
sheep	**scissors**

A Proofread Sample

Many animals' lifes depend upon hunting. Because foxs eat mouses, the two animals are natural enemys. Other animales, such as sheeps, eat only plantes.

Homophones

- When you are writing, be aware of words that sound the same but have different spellings and different meanings. The list below includes some common homophone pairs.

Homophone Pairs	
ate/eight	rain/rein/reign
bare/bear	real/reel
brake/break	root/route
dear/deer	sale/sail
dew/due	so/sew
hear/here	stationary/stationery
hole/whole	tale/tail
it's/its	to/too/two
know/no	there/their/they're
lead/led	threw/through
mail/male	vain/vein/vane
one/won	waste/waist
pair/pare/pear	wear/where
pale/pail	your/you're

A Proofread Sample

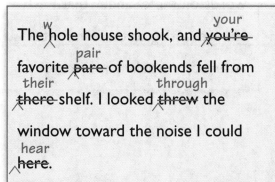

Tricky Letter Combinations

- This rhyme may help you remember to spell a word with *ei* or *ie*: "Put *i* before *e* except after *c* or when it sounds like a long *a*, as in *neighbor* and *weigh*."

believe	deceive	piece
brief	eight	receive
ceiling	field	thief
chief	niece	vein

Exceptions:

either	friend	seize
foreign	height	species
forfeit	neither	weird

- Check a dictionary or look at this list when deciding between *-sion* or *-tion* at the end of a word.

-sion	-tion
admission	action
conclusion	collection
confusion	competition
discussion	composition
division	condition
erosion	convention
explosion	description
impression	definition
invasion	pollution
vision	reaction

- Check a dictionary or look at this list when deciding between *-ant* or *-ent* at the end of a word.

-ant	-ent
accountant	absent
brilliant	absorbent
consonant	accident
constant	ancient
distant	compartment
elegant	different
ignorant	document
immigrant	efficient
important	improvement
instant	ingredient
observant	intelligent
participant	parent
pleasant	permanent
vacant	violent

Commonly Misspelled Words

- These words cause confusion mostly because writers may not know whether to use one or two consonants in them.

accelerate	discipline	misspell
accidentally	dissatisfied	necessity
accuracy	during	noticeable
address	embarrass	occasionally
already	equipment	occurrence
argument	exaggerate	pastime
ballet	experience	rebellion
balloon	galaxy	receive
calendar	grateful	recommend
category	guarantee	separated
cellar	height	summed
collectible	incidentally	twelfth
committee	intelligence	until
controlling	lightning	vacuum

A Proofread Sample

Christine could not beleive that her freind would decieve her. "It must have been an accidant!" she said. "She knew this competision was importent to me."

A Proofread Sample

It would embarass me to mispell words on the calander that I am presenting to the committe. Acurracy in spelling is a necesity.

Look for these errors in your writing (and listen for them in your speech). Try to correct them.

Subject-Verb Agreement

- The subject and the verb in a sentence must agree in number. A singular subject needs a singular verb, and a plural subject needs a plural verb. Most singular verbs in the present tense end in -s or -es.

Ella runs six miles each week.

Sometimes we run together.

- If the subject is singular, then the verb should also be singular, even if a plural noun appears between the subject and the verb.

The smell of the oranges is wonderful.

- In some questions, the verb appears before the subject.

Is it time to eat?

A Proofread Example

He ride^s his bicycle to school. We rides the bus.

Active and Passive Voice

- In the active voice, the subject performs the action.

Brandon kicks the ball.

- In the passive voice, the subject receives the action. Using the passive voice too often can make your writing awkward or confusing.

The ball is kicked by Brandon.

A Proofread Sample

Riley washed
The car was washed by Riley.

Correct Pronoun Usage

- Personal pronouns take different forms if they are the subject or object within a sentence.

Subject	Object
I	me
he/she/it	him/her/it
you	you
we	us
they	them

I mowed the lawn.

Jana helped me pull weeds.

She gave the book to him and me.

- A possessive pronoun shows that something belongs to another person or thing. Possessive pronouns do not use apostrophes to show possession.

  Is that backpack yours?

  Matt went to the movies with his brothers.

A Proofread Sample

> If the tickets are our̶'̶s, why did
>
> Theresa give them to ~~he~~? [him]

Modifiers

Adjectives and adverbs are words used to describe nouns and verbs.

Articles

- The words *a* and *an* are indefinite articles. The word *the* is a definite article.

  An animal escaped from the zoo.

Proper Adjectives

- Proper adjectives are formed from proper nouns. They are always capitalized.

  A Chicago museum displays dinosaur bones.

Adverbs

- An adverb is a word that modifies a verb, an adjective, or another adverb.

  Janelle laughed quietly.

- Many adverbs, but not all, end in *-ly*.

perfectly	**really**
always	**quite**
least	**now**
almost	**often**

Comparative and Superlative Modifiers

- Both adjectives and adverbs can be comparative or superlative. Comparative modifiers compare two people, places, things, or ideas. Superlative modifiers compare three or more.

- The comparative form ends with *-er* or is preceded by *more* (or *less*). The superlative form ends with *-est* or is preceded by *most* (or *least*).

fast	**faster**	**fastest**
quietly	**less quietly**	**least quietly**

A Proofread Sample

> Kevin stayed up ~~more late~~ [later] than
>
> Asher and Jacob, but the next
>
> morning Jacob was the ~~sleepier~~ [sleepiest] of
>
> the three boys.

Double Negatives

- Do not use two negative words together to emphasize the negative. Both of the examples below are correct, and both express the same thought.

  Angela said Phil did nothing to help her.

  Angela said Phil didn't do anything to help her.

A Proofread Sample

"Don't touch ~~nothing~~ anything until I get back," Ellen said. "I don't want ~~nobody~~ anybody else cleaning up the mess I made."

"But I can't have ~~no~~ friends over until the house is picked up," Alexander answered.

Commonly Confused Words

- **anyway, anywhere, somewhere** Do not use *anyways*, *anywheres*, or *somewheres*.

  "Where did I leave my hair dryer, anyway?" my sister asked.

  "You must have left it somewhere, but I can't find it anywhere," our mother told her.

- **bring, take** Use *bring* when the action moves toward the speaker. Use *take* when the action moves away. The past tense of *bring* is *brought*, not *brang*.

  I sometimes bring extra snacks to soccer practice. Be sure to take some if you are hungry. Last week I brought enough snacks for both teams.

- **could have, should have, must have, would have** Do not use *of* after the verbs *could*, *should*, *must*, and *would*.

  I would have gotten to school on time if I could have, but my alarm clock didn't go off. I should have remembered to plug it in last night. I must have unplugged it this weekend.

- **good, well** *Good* is always an adjective. *Well* is usually an adverb.

  "You dance extremely well," Tasha told Janet.

  "Thank you. You are a good dancer, too," Janet replied.

- **himself, themselves** Notice the correct forms of these pronouns. Do not use *hisself* or *theirselves*.

  My older brother is always looking in the mirror, so he must be very fond of himself.

  They kept the news to themselves.

- **reason is because** Use either *the reason is* or *because*, not both together.

  The reason I finished my homework early is that I wanted to see my favorite TV show.

  I finished my homework early because I wanted to see my favorite TV show.

- **lay, lie** Do not use *lay* when you mean *lie*. *Lie* means "to rest or recline." *Lay* means "to place or set." These two verbs are challenging for many writers, so check a dictionary or the examples and the chart below if you are uncertain about which to use.

  My dog knows many commands, including "sit," "roll over," and "lie down."

  The game is over, so it's time to lay your cards on the table.

- **their, there, they're** *Their* is a possessive pronoun that means "belonging to them." *There* is an adverb that describes location. *They're* is a contraction of "they are."

  The softball players are looking for their bats and mitts. Please tell them that they're over there.

- **to, too, two** *To* is an adverb. *Too* is an adverb that means "very" or "also." *Two* is the number 2.

  Two pizzas are too many for my family to eat.

  We're going to Wisconsin for two weeks next summer. You can come, too.

Lay and Lie				
Verb	**Present Participle**	**Past Tense**	**Past Participle**	**Examples**
lie ("to rest or recline"; does not take an object)	lying	lay	(has) lain	If you are tired, please lie down. I was lying down this morning. I lay on the couch yesterday. My cat has lain on the floor all afternoon.
lay ("to place or set"; laying takes an object)	laying	laid	(has) laid	Sometimes I lay a trap for my brother. He is smart, so laying a trap for him is difficult. He laid one for me last Tuesday, and he has often laid traps for my sister and me in the past.

Index